Tangled

A SOUL CARE GUIDE TO REMOVE THE WEEDS IN OUR LIVES AND PLANT LIFE-GIVING SEEDS

WHY?

We want deep roots when the storms of life come.
We want to live free from the sin that so easily entangles.
We want to live an abundant and joyful life.

"For what you plant will always be the very thing you harvest. The harvest you reap reveals the seed that was planted. If you plant the corrupt seeds of self-life into this natural realm, you can expect to experience a harvest of corruption. If you plant the good seeds of Spirit-life you will reap the beautiful fruits that grow from the everlasting life of the Spirit."

GALATIANS 6:7-8 (TPT)

Introduction

Headphones, Christmas lights, necklaces... set them down and the experience is the same. Tangled.

"But how do they possibly get tangled so easily?" I constantly asked myself this question as my fingers worked to unwrap and unwind the cord. I was so frustrated every time I threw my headphones into my purse only to retrieve them in a knotted heap. It was as if there was a magical purse fairy whose sole job was to jumble up this cord! (I also blame the purse fairy for the smattering of receipts, hair ties, old tissues and candy wrappers.)

The tangling is confusing. It is perplexing. It is frustrating. And it happens EVERY SINGLE TIME! Also - I have tried those retractable headphones - nope, they are super annoying. Yes and I know there are wireless headphones, but I just sent my husband's through the wash so it's a bit of a sensitive topic around here...

Thankfully this book is not about headphones, though the 'tangled' I see in the world isn't that different. I see it everywhere. People walking around empty, hurting, anxiety-ridden, depressed, and purpose-less. I also see the ways in which people try to hide their 'tangling.' My ears perk up when I hear someone describe a particular quirk they have learned to live with and quickly say "but it's no big deal" or "but everyone thinks that way or struggles with that right?"

When you're tangled you find comfort in others who are tangled like you. It makes this whole thing feel less scary and isolating. As the saying goes, "Misery loves company." And while having a buddy or a 'tribe' that is going through similar life circumstances or shares similar viewpoints isn't a bad thing per se, it just doesn't help you get 'un-tangled.' In fact, some of our buddies keep us even more tangled by affirming for us that our current state and thought patterns are okay, claiming that this is "just life." And maybe they offer helpful suggestions as to how to cope with our issues. Maybe they suggest distraction through Netflix or a girl's night out. Maybe they offer a new way of eating or exercising, suggest a class to take or provide comfort in the way of food and drink. (Though we usually don't need a friend to help us find those answers.) Again, not all of those suggestions are harmful - but they are often more a means of coping, covering up, distracting, and in some ways solidifying where we are instead of helping us get the freedom our heart truly longs for.

I notice the tangling because I too once occupied that space as a form of 'normal' life. For the longest time I didn't know why. I couldn't understand the mystery. I often wondered "Is this how life will always be? Is this just who I am?" This book was birthed through my experience of God unwinding the tangles in my life and the freedom that has come through this unraveling. Unraveling seems to have a negative connotation. But what if it's the best thing to ever happen to you? A letting go. A freeing.

Call the Doctor!

I used to read this passage and think "Phew! Glad that's not me! Glad I'm the healthy one!" Every time I read this passage or others like this; I was always relieved to know that I didn't need the doctor. I was saved. "Woo hoo! Now let's go help those who don't know Him!"

Imagine my surprise when I realized that it was I all along who needed the doctor - and still do. Yes, I am saved. Gloriously, freely and truly saved. But I am still human. Darn! And my human condition means I am prone to sin. I am prone to screw up no matter how "good" I am and how hard I try.

It's okay though. It's actually kind of relieving. You see, once you are aware of your disease, you can get help for it. I had been walking through life with all of these awful symptoms yet didn't know why. I thought my condition was called "life" and that this was just how it was. So yes, I am the sick, and yes, I need a doctor, but I am not at all upset about it. I am thankful that I know the 'Great Physician' and that He does house calls.

"Now there is in Jerusalem by the Sheep Gate a pool, in Aramaic called Bethesda, which has five roofed colonnades. In these lay a multitude of invalids - blind, lame, and paralyzed. One man was there who had been an invalid for thirty-eight years. When Jesus saw him lying there and knew that he had already been there a long time, he said to him, "Do you want to be healed?" The sick man answered him, "Sir, I have no one to put me into the pool when the water is stirred up, and while I am going another steps down before me." Jesus said to him,

I love this passage because I see so much of myself in it. For years, I was the one lying by the pool hoping someone would come along to rescue me. I just laid there passively, blaming all the people around me for the state of my condition; my husband, my children, my finances, my work, my geography. I hadn't done anything wrong, I was a victim to my own life, lying there helpless. And as we will see in weeks to come that is exactly where the enemy wants us, in a helpless, hopeless state; paralyzed and unable to rise up. And yes, in moments of despair I prayed, "Jesus, save me from my anxiety and depression." But you see, just as He asked the man lying by the pool at Bethesda, He is asking us "Do you want to be healed?" Jesus is *wanting* us to participate and partner with Him in our full restoration. Yes, He has the power to do all things regardless of our cooperation but so often I think He is asking us because the issues we often pray for are merely those on the surface, as painful as they may be, but He wants to deal with the deeper matters of the heart.

He already knows what our real condition is, even more so than we do. But we can't just lay around passively hoping for healing and restoration to take place without our cooperation. He performs the heart transformation and He is the ultimate healer; however, we need to take action. We need to get up, take up our bed, and walk.

This is our call to action: *For us to stop waiting for someone to rescue us and to partner with our Creator to be fully restored into who He wants us to be.*

What to Expect

This is a 6-week study and here is what you can expect each week:

Week 1 - *Assess the Soil*: What are weeds? How are they planted?

Week 2 - *Digging Deeper:* How do we identify the weeds in our life?

Week 3 - *Uprooting:* How do we get rid of weeds?

Week 4 - *Planting*: Sow what you want to grow.

Week 5 - *Sustaining*: Strengthening your garden and growing deep roots for when the storms of life come.

Week 6 - *Maintaining*: Prevent weeds from growing, and continue to weed, daily, weekly, and seasonally.

Each week will include a short lesson, followed by discussion questions. If you are able to do this portion in a group, I think you will experience greater encouragement, accountability and deeper understanding of the material. So, grab some girlfriends and take this journey together!

The last portion is your Lifework, very similar to homework but much more life-giving. THIS is where the real transformation takes place. No one can do this work for you, and no one will make the time for you to do it. Just like the man sitting by the pool in Bethesda, this is where you ask yourself "do I want to get well?" So, I encourage you to plan out time in your calendar and make this a priority.

I have also included a weekly song, as music is such a powerful tool to help us process life and connect with our emotions.

I wanted to include a song for this introduction as well to remind us that regardless of where we are at, God longs to rescue us. Feel free to pause where you are and using whatever method you access music find "Rescue" by Lauren Daigle[1].

Simply close your eyes and listen. Know that wherever you find yourself, God is on a mission to rescue you - from your hurt, your pain, your anxious thoughts; wherever you find yourself Tangled.

Words of Encouragement

Have you ever done something part-way and then later on wished you had done it all the way? I once watched a girl at summer camp climb up the "Tower of Terror" telephone pole painfully slowly and then sit partway in agony before tearfully making her descent. Listening to her that night as we sat around the cabin talking, she was so incredibly disappointed with herself and the fact that she wasn't able to finish what she had started. I too was frustrated as I was her leader. I had allowed other well-meaning voices to drown out my cheering her on towards the top. These other voices told her she should be happy with half-way and it was fine for her to come down. I knew the disappointment she felt would far outweigh any fear she felt in climbing. And I also knew the joy and freedom she would experience if she was able to conquer this task.

Thankfully she was given a second chance the following day. And even though she was terrified each step of the way, she conquered her fear, she climbed to the top of the "Tower." And as her feet touched the ground after her success, the deep sense of joy she felt was palpable. I tell you this story because this will not be easy. Facing our real issues head-on is not light work. There are things in your life that have been buried a long time and bringing them to the surface can be painful. It is much easier to avoid things that are hard, scary and like the top of the "Tower," can feel shaky. However, the feeling of joy you will have once your feet touch ground will be worth it!

So, commit to completing each week of this course and especially to the Lifework. The work that Jesus wants to do in your heart so often takes place when we meet Him face-to-face, one-on-one. That is where we really become un-tangled.

Tending the Soil

A friend of mine recently took an "Organic Master Gardening" course. In her words, "When your plant is unhealthy or being attacked by insects, instead of treating the symptoms, for example, spraying an insecticide to get rid of bugs, *you need to address the source of the plant's health, which is the soil.* When the soil is full of nutrients and organic matter is feeding the microbes, your soil is teeming with life. The plants get what they need to be healthy and the pests bypass the healthy plant and attack those that are weak. *Different weeds in your soil will indicate certain deficiencies in your soil, as will diseases."* *Zipporah Hanke*[2]

And that is what we are going to do in this study: tend to the soil (soul).

Assess the Soil

I don't think it's a coincidence that all of humanity began in a garden. Close your eyes and picture the most beautiful garden you could ever imagine. Flowers in full bloom, their sweet intoxicating scent almost overpowering your senses. Birds chirping, a light breeze blowing, the sky is blue and the sun is shining brightly. THIS! THIS is what God intended for us. Genesis 2:25 tells us *"Adam and his wife were both naked, and they felt no shame."* They were living with full hearts light and free. But when sin entered the world, that peace was stripped away. Mimicking the inner shame that now grew in Adam and Eve's hearts, the ground began to produce thorns and thistles. No longer were Adam and Eve living in peace - they allowed sin into their hearts and this began humanity's struggle with contentment.

VERSE OF THE WEEK

"Search me, God, and know my heart; test me and know my anxious thoughts. See if there is any offensive way in me, and lead me in the way everlasting."

PSALM 139:23-24

Soil

I love when auto-correct sheds light on things for me. I typed soil into my phone but looked down to instead see the word soul. And in this case "auto-correct" couldn't be more correct. We are going to be looking at the soil of our hearts which is essentially our soul.

My question for you as we begin is this: how is your soil? Or to put it another way - how is your soul?

Hands up if you are a gardener? I am not! I am embarrassed to say that my mom has often come to my house, weeded my garden, bought the flowers, and planted them for me. My job then was to just keep everything alive! (A job I often failed!) Keep in mind I have had 3 summer babies and a giant pregnant belly plus bending over generally do not mesh well!

In the last few years however, I have tried to make more of an effort to do the weeding, purchasing and planting myself. But the problem I have is that I don't always know the difference *between* a weed or a plant.

Sometimes I actually think the weeds look kind of pretty. We had one huge weed last year that I didn't even bother uprooting. It was giant and had purple flowers at the top. Besides, for a weed to be that big you *know* the roots would be HUGE! And *so* difficult to pull out.

Have you ever tried to get rid of a really big weed? First, it's important to have the right tools. Just using your hands is nearly impossible. A good weed tool is essential. I'm sure they have names, but I just call them "weed tools." Secondly you need to make sure you get rid of the ENTIRE weed - roots and all. Otherwise, it just grows back! And I don't know if the theory on "pluck one grey hair and two grow back" also applies to weeds but I think so! They are relentless, nearly unstoppable, they have no boundaries or respect for your other plants. In fact, one of their jobs it seems is to choke out other flowers, the good ones, the ones you paid for and planted! They can get in the way of those flowers blooming well. They can even stop them from blooming at all!

Weeds are the worst. They tangle, they choke out, they steal the beauty you are trying to achieve in your garden. But like I already mentioned, they are tricky. If you aren't an experienced gardener you won't know what to pull out. And you might, like me, leave a weed *just because it is sort of pretty*.

Even if you're not a savvy gardener, or have never planted anything in the ground, hopefully you will be able to follow along with me when I say *we are all planting seeds in the soil of our hearts.*

And those seeds can either grow life, or they can grow weeds.

The sneaky thing about the weeds in our life (our heart, our soul - soil) is that they're often planted without us realizing it, or without us being *consciously* aware. They also can be unassuming or even look pretty, but their effects on our soul can be devastating.

In the past I was often frustrated thinking, "I'm a Christian. I am a new creation. Why then do I feel depressed? Why am I so angry all the time? Why do I not have joy? Is this how life is meant to be? I thought life with Christ was supposed to be abundant and free? Why do I feel so tangled?"

Our Gardens

One afternoon I sat down at the request of my daughter to colour. I approached the blank white sheet of paper and began to draw a garden. My artistic skills peaked at grade three so it was quite basic. But as each flower bloomed, I realized I have a garden in my heart and I have not been planting what I want to see grow. I was planting bitterness and anger but hoping for joy. I was planting resentment and jealousy but hoping for love and self-control. I was planting fear and anxiety but hoping for peace.

I wrote at the top of the page, "Plant What You Want to See Grow." Nothing too profound, but it spoke to me. *If I want to live a life of joy and peace, I need to pay attention to what is being planted.*

Our theme verse for this book is from Galatians 6:7-8. I love the wording from The Passion Translation.

> *"For what you plant will always be the very thing you harvest. The harvest you reap reveals the seed that was planted. If you plant the corrupt seeds of self-life into this natural realm, you can expect to experience a harvest of corruption. If you plant the good seeds of Spirit-life you will reap the beautiful fruits that grow from the everlasting life of the Spirit."*
> **GALATIANS 6:7-8 (TPT)**

As I began to look even closer at the soil of my heart, I began to see how I had planted weeds, others had planted weeds, and the enemy had planted weeds. So, it wasn't all my fault!! But I also began to see that, regardless of who had done the planting, I had cultivated these weeds. *I began to see how I had tended them with my words, my attitudes and my behaviours.*

You may be thinking, "Well that's not me! Why am I reading this study?" But stick with me. I want to show you what the weeds in your life are and how to uproot them. I want you to experience the freedom of living an untangled life.

As a novice gardener I have had to rely on my mom to help me identify the weeds in my garden. I have also needed the help of my husband or dad to help remove a particularly large weed. The same is true for us in our hearts. We need the Holy Spirit to tell us where the weeds lie in our hearts and we need His help to remove them. When we try to be "good gardeners" on our own we often can't fully remove the weed, and when roots are left behind it will simply grow again.

Weeds

We're spending the first half of this study simply looking at the weeds in our hearts, learning to identify them and uproot them. While this doesn't mean you can't begin to plant the good things you want to grow, we first want to create a really beautiful foundation.

As hard as it is to say, I believe we all have secret soul sins that are entangling us and keeping us from living our fullest joy-filled lives. As a little kid you quickly learn to hide the things you are ashamed of. Who told you it was better to keep secrets to yourself than to bring them into the light? No one had to tell you. Buried deep within us is a human nature to be in control, to self-preserve, and to keep ourselves from the consequences we believe will face us when we bring our darkness into the light.

What we fail to realize is that hiding our darkness is one of the ways the enemy entangles us.

There is freedom in the light. There is also possibly a bit of pain as those things are exposed, but never shame. Shame is not God's plan for us. The enemy tries to attach shame to what we have done as a means of keeping us stuck. If he can trick us into thinking we are better off burying things deep within our heart he can continue to attach other things to that place. Things like lies, fear, depression, anxiety, jealousy, self-pity, bitterness, unforgiveness, and anger. When we are able to find freedom from the things that so easily entangle us the enemy doesn't have any ground to attach his weeds. And this isn't anything new, he's been doing this since the beginning of time.

Let's go back to the original garden:

> *"Adam and his wife were both naked, and they felt no shame."*
> **GENESIS 2:25**

> *"Now the serpent was more crafty than any of the wild animals the Lord God had made. He said to the woman, "Did God really say, 'You must not eat from any tree in the garden'?"*
> **GENESIS 3:1**

> *"Then the eyes of both of them were opened, and they realized they were naked; so they sewed fig leaves together and made coverings for themselves. Then the man and his wife heard the sound of the Lord God as he was walking in the garden in the cool of the day, and they hid from the Lord God among the trees of the garden."*
> **GENESIS 3:7-8**

Let's break it down for a minute:

Adam and Eve felt no shame. Then sin entered the world - through the serpent. (There was no shame until sin entered the picture). His first question to Eve was, *"Did God really say?"*

He *plants a seed of doubt* which, through their actions, produces a weed of shame. Adam and Eve watered those seeds through their secrecy, hiding from God. The sin that began as a tiny seed burst forth full bloom into a weed of regret and a consequence of life outside the garden.

We are human. We are prone to screw up. *And when we choose to hide those screw ups from God instead of bringing them into the light through confession and repentance their roots are strengthened making them difficult to get rid of.*

Fast forward many years and Jesus is now on the scene to once and for all destroy sin AND shame. And He does, in the most beautiful, sacrificial display of love that humanity has ever seen. He destroys everything intended to separate us from the love of the Father and ensure our salvation. He endured the *shame* of the cross *for us*. To *remove* our shame. Yet, many of us still carry around shame as if Jesus did not destroy it for us. We may have tried to shake it off but felt like it's stuck to us like sap from a tree. You can scrub and scrub and scrub but it seems impossible to remove.

I had an experience awhile back. I knew I had not behaved in a way that I wanted to. I knew my actions did not line up with who I felt Jesus was calling me to be. I woke up the next morning and felt immense shame. I also felt disqualified. Whatever good God had been doing in my life until that point felt destroyed. My gut response was to give up. To lie down in my shame and declare my life worthless. But I tried something new.

Instead of hiding in my sin and shame I went to Him.

I closed my eyes in prayer and was surprised when I saw myself walking in the woods by my house. I am not a particularly visual person when it comes to prayer so this was a rare moment. As I walked along, I was shocked to see Jesus walking towards me. As He got closer, I began to brace myself. Surely, He would have something to say about my behaviour. I could feel my body begin to curl as I anticipated hearing the words "I didn't die on the cross for you to behave this way!" He got closer and I stopped, and waited. Then I felt it. He leaned in and wrapped His arms around me. He held me close with a compassionate, Fatherly, embrace.

As we parted and stepped back, I looked down. I noticed a bag beside His feet. And as He bent down to pick this bag up, I saw in big, bold writing the word SHAME written across its side. He flung the bag over His shoulder and began to walk away. I started to weep. I had known God my entire life, but I didn't know this.

His desire is not to condemn us or to shame us. As things come up for us when we begin to weed, it is simply so He can pick it up and carry it away.

"For God did not send his Son into the world to condemn the world, but to save the world through him."

JOHN 3:17

How Weeds are Planted

I don't know about you but I have never intentionally planted a weed in my front yard. Yet, year after year they appear. The way they are planted is a mystery. And looking at the soil of our hearts can seem just as confusing. How did those weeds get there? And for some of the weeds in the soil of our heart, we may never know the answer. But I have found there are three main ways in which weeds tend to get planted in our lives: we plant seeds, others plant seeds, and the enemy plants seeds.

The other tricky thing about weeds is that the seed may be planted in our hearts, but we sometimes don't see the evidence of that weed until much later. This makes identifying the source tricky. If I spend my evenings scrolling social media and consuming images of other people's lives I will start to feel discontent with my own. This may not happen right away, but as I continue to plant seeds of comparison, I will begin to see weeds of jealousy and envy spring up over time. The negative words spoken over us as children may not seem to affect us as we are growing up, but years later when we become mothers, that weed may seem to spring up overnight. The trickiest of all are the weeds planted by the enemy. He is an expert in planting seeds throughout our lives through comments and actions made by others, misunderstandings, and offences. He holds his cards tight and then when we are in a vulnerable moment, he will play a strategic weed against us to keep us tangled and confused about who we are truly meant to be.

We Plant Seeds

This was a shock to me. I didn't really ever give much thought to the consequences of my actions. As I said earlier, this is partly because the consequences don't always show up immediately. Have you ever warned a child that "If you watch that scary show you might get nightmares." We understand this as a parent. What you put into your mind now will affect you later. So why do we have so much trouble understanding this as adults?

All day long we are planting seeds through the words we say, what we watch, listen to, and what we participate in. Our social media accounts have a news "feed" and we are being 'fed' daily.

We hear of a tragic news story and then we seek out more to read about this event. Being informed is not a bad thing, but sometimes we are feeding ourselves fear and anxiety. We shouldn't be surprised when that is what we reap. I don't know about you, but often when I hear of a tragedy my brain begins to believe the same thing will happen to me and my loved ones. We are *planting seeds of fear* - which in turn grow *weeds of anxiety.*

We feed our souls beautiful pictures of others living their 'best life,' *planting seeds of comparison,* resulting in *weeds of jealousy and self-pity.* For a long time, I was addicted to reality TV shows where women were portrayed as having glamorous lives, but would spend most of their time fighting over petty disagreements. I was *planting seeds of discontent* in my life looking at all that they had, and *seeds of anger* simply listening to them argue.

As we begin to identify the ways in which we plant seeds in our lives I have found two things to be helpful. We need to: 1) Be aware 2) Get out of a victim mindset.

1) Be Aware: We are believing a lie if we feel like we are somehow immune to what we read, watch, and participate in.

Growing up I heard a version of the quote "If you want to know who you will be in five years, look at the books you read, the shows you watch and who you are surrounding yourself with." At the time, five years seemed like an eternity! Now that I am a little older, I can see this to be incredibly true. I am planting seeds each and every day through my actions, my conversations, and what I consume. The results of these little seeds don't immediately produce fruit but I am cultivating what I want in my life through each of these choices.

I am that person that never orders a salad at a restaurant. I will sit down with the best of intentions but by the time I finish scanning the menu I have likely picked a fully-loaded juicy burger and crispy, hot fries. I want the thing that I know will leave me satisfied. I don't trust that the salad will do the job. But here's the thing. If I went an entire year picking the burger and fries every day my body would begin to take on a new shape. Not right away. I wouldn't notice the first day, and there wouldn't be much of a change the first week. But making that same choice day after day would begin to affect me. The same is true for the salad choice. If I made the "healthy" choice day after day I also may not see a result right away. But a year into the process I would notice.

And we get that on a purely physical level. It's easy to see how the example of eating has an effect on my body but somehow, *we forget that we are feeding our souls daily as well.*

> "Do you not know that you are God's temple and that God's Spirit dwells in you? If anyone destroys God's temple, God will destroy him. For God's temple is holy, and you are that temple."
>
> **1 CORINTHIANS 3:16-17 (ESV)**

Hmm, well that sounds serious. I used to read that verse and sort of freak out. Kind of like a "Well it's all over now, I've screwed up already!" Then I began to read the Old Testament. I began to see the bigger picture of who God is and the relationship He had with His chosen people, the Israelites. To make a long story short, they continued to turn away from God, which evoked His anger, but He always had a plan to draw them back to Him. This is our God. Regardless of what we have done, He wants to draw us back to Him. I love the verse in Haggai that talks about the physical rebuilding of God's temple.

> "The glory of this present house will be greater than the glory of the former house,' says the Lord Almighty. 'And in this place I will grant peace,' declares the LORD Almighty."
>
> **HAGGAI 2:9**

I believe this is absolutely true for us as well. The glory God wants to reveal in you will be greater than what you have previously been, and He will grant you peace. What a beautiful picture.

And this same verse in The Message version:

"'This Temple is going to end up far better than it started out, a glorious beginning but an even more glorious finish: a place in which I will hand out wholeness and holiness.' Decree of God-of-the-Angel-Armies."

Wholeness. Isn't that what we all want? Deep peace, fullness of life, and wholeness. And this is what God longs to do in our lives. Regardless of where we are at. Regardless of what we have done. He longs to bring us to full restoration.

2) Victim Mindset: When we blame others for what is happening to us, we put ourselves in a victim mindset.

As victims we become helpless, hopeless and powerless and this is exactly where the enemy wants us (more on that later). I am not talking about what others have actually done to us, I am talking about the things that we are blaming others for. There are many things we simply cannot control such as what has happened in our past, and what other people do. When we are able to realize there is *a difference between what we can control and what we can't*, we begin to stand up and take responsibility for *our own thoughts, words, and actions*.

I used to blame my kids for the grumpiness I felt. They would often wake me up in the middle of the night so they were an easy target for my arrow of blame. And while yes, the disrupted sleep did contribute to my 'feelings' of grumpiness, it wasn't really their fault. My grumpiness was still ultimately my choice. I could choose be tired and happy, or tired and miserable. I simply chose the easy way out by saying "You did this to me." The fact remains that sleep or no sleep I would still likely be grumpy. Once I was aware of this and could take ownership of it, I was able to work on shifting my mindset away from grumpiness to feeling content.

Tying my happiness to their behaviour kept me stuck in
a cycle of blame and chained me to grumpiness.

There is power in being aware of what you can and cannot control. It is freeing. When I begin to realize that I don't have to rely on other people to dictate my emotions, I am able to have more control over them and make better decisions. I am able to be responsible for my own life. I once again have a say in my life instead of being a victim to it.

As I shared in the introduction, Jesus asked the man in Bethesda, "Do you want to get well?" For many of us we have been living with a victim mindset waiting for someone to heal us instead of realizing we need to renew our mind and take action. Jesus does not leave us where we are. He offers us His hand and says "Get up! Let's do this. Do you want to get well?"

Others Plant Seeds

Others plant seeds in us through the words they say over us, what they may have said to us when we were children, and what they have done to us.

This may be one of the reasons some of us have a victim mindset. Maybe you have been a victim; of verbal abuse, emotional abuse, physical abuse, or sexual abuse. Depending on the nature and severity of this abuse there may be a need for counselling. And I hope you know this but I will say it to be certain. There is wisdom in seeking out someone to help work through the issues of pain and suffering you may have endured at the hands of another person. There is great healing that can come when we are able to bring our hurt to light while someone we trust walks alongside us. If there is anything that has come to mind as I've spoken these words, I would suggest the additional Lifework of seeking out someone to walk alongside you in this area.

I also want to talk about the ways in which others can plant seeds in seemingly less harmful ways, and sometimes in ways they were unaware of. Was there something friends or family said to you or about you when you were a child? We are shaped and molded by the words we hear, especially during our formative stages. At this point in our life hopefully we are able to discern truth from a lie, but when we are children and teenagers, we often don't have the skills to filter these things and instead take them in. They become who we believe we are, and many times we have embraced lies for truth.

I'm going to pause here for a moment and if something has come to mind, as silly or as small as it might seem, that is part of the Holy Spirit prompting our hearts. If you had a memory, a thought or a picture - take a moment to write that down.

Sometimes the lies we have believed have a very simple origin. Not all of the harm done by others was intentional, and not all was done in malice.

But the enemy has a way of twisting our experiences, especially in our formative years, into lies to keep us in bondage.

For many women I have spoken to well into their 50's and 60's they have had a memory from childhood that has shaped what they have believed about themselves. As they have spent a moment re-visiting this experience alongside the Holy Spirit, they have been able to see it for what it was and have been able to find freedom from this lie that has been holding them hostage.

For me, a silly example is about my birthday. Every year on my birthday I would experience a time of loneliness, feeling sorry for myself and often tears. This past year as my husband and I began to discuss my upcoming birthday, I noticed my chest begin to tighten and that I had trouble breathing. Why would my birthday evoke such negative emotions?

As a child with a summer birthday I often had very small parties. My friends would be out of town on vacation and sometimes the party consisted of a few neighbourhood boys my parents could round up. I did not think much of this at all.

As we sat down to unpack this together, we realized that I had a deep association between my birthday and feeling like I had no friends. This was simply not true. It was a lie. But because this lie was planted over 30 years ago it had deep roots. I had to let go of this lie and replace it with the truth. I do have friends. Yes, many of them still go on vacation during my birthday, but it does not negate our friendship or leave me unworthy of friendship. I could not believe the freedom that came from being released from this lie.

The Holy Spirit continues to identify the lies in my life, often using my emotions as a guide. "Why am I reacting that way?" "Why is that emotion coming up so strongly?"

Sometimes the emotion released is through tears, sometimes anger, sometimes it is a reaction in a moment that seems unexpected or not "normal."

So, what does the soil of our heart look like? To truly assess the soil of our heart we need to ask the Holy Spirit for help. We will use this week's theme verse to pray *"Search me, God, and know my heart; test me and know my anxious thoughts. See if there is any offensive way in me, and lead me in the way everlasting." Psalm 139:23-24*

This week's Lifework will include some time of solitude and prayer where you can ask the Holy Spirit this very question. Search my heart God, or as it says in the Message version *"See for yourself whether I've done anything wrong - then guide me on the road to eternal life."*

Let's stop here for now. I think there is enough to process in terms of assessing our soil. Next week we will discuss the way the enemy plants seeds.

SONG: *"Wonderfully Made"* by Ellie Holcomb[3]

DISCUSSION QUESTIONS:

1) Rate the soil of your heart: a) Fertilized and blooming b) Not bad but could use some pruning and weeding c) A disaster zone. If you can, explain why.

2) The serpent asked Eve "Did God really say?" Where is one area you have experienced a seed of doubt or discouragement in your life? Write down words of truth to combat this seed.

3) For our Lifework this week you will *Assess your Soil*. Pull out your calendar and plan a 1-2 hour window for this quiet time. Right now, decide on where that will be and come up with an outdoor and an indoor option where you can be totally alone. Write down that time and place here! You will need your Bible, this book, possibly a journal, and some worship music. I like music to help prepare my heart to hear from God but I would also encourage you to just sit in the silence of the moment.

LIFEWORK:

Assess your soil - Set aside time to be still before God and talk together about your heart soil. (Give yourself 1-2 hours of uninterrupted time to make the most of this Lifework)

1) As you meet with God, pray aloud Psalm 139:24

> *"Search me, God, and know my heart; test me and know my anxious thoughts. See if there is any offensive way in me, and lead me in the way everlasting."*
> **PSALM 139:24**

This is a good time to really be still, time to turn off the music and just listen. What is God saying to your heart? Condemning words that produce anxiety, fear, or confusion are not from God. (Remember the serpent in the garden).

This may not be an easy time my friend. Though God's words are not condemning sometimes when we become aware of the weeds in our heart it can feel painful, emotional, and we can experience guilt, shame and sadness. Know that although God wants you to be aware of these things it is simply so you can partner with Him in their removal. Not for you to sit in a place of pain. As I have walked through this process in my own life, I have often felt a physical pain in the left side of my body where my heart is. I will feel God scraping away what He never intended to be there. Not to mix metaphors but God is the ultimate heart surgeon and He is so gentle. He does not want to harm you in this process but sometimes the removal of weeds will produce a bit of pain as we become aware of what is in our heart and begin to surrender these things to Him.

2) Are there any weeds He would like to remove? If He reveals anything to you give Him that weed.

"Therefore, since we have these promises, dear friends, let us purify ourselves from everything that contaminates body and spirit, perfecting holiness out of reverence for God."
2 CORINTHIANS 7:1

Although it might feel a bit painful don't rush this process. Take the time to allow God to guide your heart and mind. Continue to release to Him anything that comes to mind, regardless of how trivial it may seem. Allow yourself to feel your pain and emotions and know that this is part of the healing process. We are cultivating our soil. One of the definitions of cultivate means to "break up (soil) in preparation for sowing or planting."[4] Before we can plant the garden God desires for us, we need to begin to uproot.

"We are coworkers with God and you are God's cultivated garden, the house he is building."
1 CORINTHIANS 3:9 (TPT)

3) The first section of Psalm 139 proclaims how well God knows us, and it goes on to explain that it is because He created us inside our mother's womb. Near the end it begins to talk about enemies and for many of us (hopefully) we can't really think of a true "enemy" in our lives. At least no one we would be asking God to "slay" as it says in vs 19. If you read this section understanding there is an enemy of our souls it makes a little more sense who our true enemy is and why we would want God's help to be rid of this enemy. *Read all of Psalm 139 out loud.*

4) Listen to *"Wonderfully Made"* by Ellie Holcomb[5]. Let the words wash over you and know the truth that our amazing Creator made YOU and loves you more than words can express. "What if I saw me the way that you see me."

For some of us, this is hard to believe. We have grown up believing lies about who we are, that we are flawed, that we are damaged and broken beyond repair. As you listen to these lyrics, even if you struggle to believe them as truth, try and take them in. Take note of any emotions you experience. Is there anything you have trouble believing about yourself? Jot those down. Take them to Him as you sit. Why are you feeling these emotions? Why do you believe what you do about yourself? God's hope is for you to know,

> *"You are altogether beautiful, my darling; there is no flaw in you."*
> **SONG OF SONGS 4:7**

Part of the untangling is beginning to believe we are who God says we are, and begin to drop the lies about what others have said about who we are. Often this is a process. Do not be hard on yourself if you don't "feel" a certain way right away. The un-tangling can take time, but you are moving in the right direction.

I am excited to dive a little deeper this week into our study. I am hoping you were able to spend some time assessing the soil of your heart. It is so hard to know where to begin if we are not first aware of where we are. A lot of the time it starts with being honest with ourselves. I heard recently that the worst person you can try to deceive is yourself. If for some reason you did not get last week's Lifework done please make that a priority first thing this week.

This week's theme is Digging Deeper. Last week I mentioned that it is hard sometimes to tell the difference between a plant and a weed. And one of the reasons it's so difficult is that weeds often grow pretty leaves or flowers. My kids are thrilled with weeds. "You mean, I can just pick this yellow flower from any patch of grass at any time?!" It's like they've won the flower lottery. I have received more dandelions from my kids than I could ever possibly hope for. I am the worst and don't even pretend to keep them for the duration of the walk, they always seem to go missing before we get home!

Even though my children are master dandelion pickers they are not actually removing the weeds. They are picking off the flower, but leaving the roots intact. If I really want to deal with a weed problem, I have to remove the weed at the source, the root. Last week we had an assessment of our soil, and this week we are going even deeper, really trying to get to the roots. We want to yank out the weeds completely so they do not grow back.

VERSE OF THE WEEK

"For God will never give you the spirit of fear, but the Holy Spirit who gives you mighty power, love, and self-control."

2 TIMOTHY 1:7 (TPT)

Weed Identification

How do I begin to identify a weed? I have found one of the best places to start with weed identification is to pay attention to my emotions. Even though our emotions are terrible masters they are not all bad. Our emotions can be like a neon sign pointing us to the fact that something isn't right. As long as we can see them as a sign *directing* us to the root of the issue our emotions can be one of our best tools in weed identification. However, when we allow our emotions to rule us or become *the issue* we are no longer able to identify the root of the problem because we will be *distracted* by the flower on top of the weed. Sort of like focusing on a symptom rather than the actual issue.

Let's say for example, I realize I am having an emotional response to a topic that has come up. I may choose fight or flight depending on the situation. I may want to run away from it. Or I may want to *defend* the way I'm feeling about this topic. Either way I am ignoring the red flag that says "Wow I am becoming incredibly emotional about this. Is *this* really the issue or is there a root issue?"

When we can take our emotional response to a situation and pause while we hold a mirror to our heart it helps us identify and deal with the root.

Recently I had a friend ask a simple favour of me. Immediately I wanted to refuse because she had declined helping me in a similar way a few months prior. When she refused a few months ago I allowed a seed of bitterness to plant itself in my heart instead of just taking her "no" at face value which was that she was simply too busy to say "yes." Rather than appreciating that she was giving a healthy "no" to protect herself from burning out I took it as a personal slight. She refused to help me in my time of need! (In my mind anyways.) It wasn't a huge deal and I verbalized that to myself. *But the heart issue is always the one to deal with.* Even though I have seen her many times since and never consciously thought of this issue, once she asked me a similar favour the emotions of the past flared up.

I was then left with a choice; do I help her or do I say "no" out of spite? And while that is the issue on the surface, (the flower/the distraction) in order to uproot the weed of bitterness that was planted I needed to address the actual issue. Thankfully, I can credit my emotions for triggering that there was a seed of bitterness planted at all.

Many weeds will lay dormant until an emotional response to a conversation or circumstance shoots them to the surface. When we can use this emotional response to point us to the root of the issue - we can deal with it.

In the case of my friend I could choose to discuss it with her. (I am a huge fan of crucial conversations to clear up any miscommunications between friends.) But sometimes while I am in the process of weed removal, I am still a little too emotional to speak as clearly as I need to without contributing to greater miscommunication and possibly more hurt. Often what I need to do is simply take it to God. He's the one that helped me identify the seed of bitterness. I can go to Him, confess this weed and ask Him to fully remove it and ask that He plant love for my friend in its place. Then whether I choose to say yes or no to her request for help I can do so, not from a place of bitterness or obligation, but out of love for my friend and myself.

It takes a lot of self-control and willpower to choose to seek out the root of the issue instead of fight or flight. Fight or flight is instinctual, and likely it is how we have always operated. However, we are learning a new operating system, one that is dependent on Jesus for everything. We are undergoing a heart renovation with Him as the master surgeon (or gardener to stick with our analogy).

Our theme verse for this week says *"For God will never give you the spirit of fear, but the Holy Spirit who gives you mighty power, love, and self-control." 2 Timothy 1:7 (TPT).* On my own I do not have the self-control required to get to the root of the weeds in my life when they present themselves. But when I yield to Him, when I surrender and ask for His help to have the self-control and perseverance to deal with the weeds in my life, He will give it, it is a promise we can stand on.

When our emotions point to a weed in our life and we are able to choose to deal with it instead of our natural fight or flight response that is when we can begin to identify the root. It doesn't come naturally and it's not easy; this is where the real heart work will take place. And once that weed is removed you will be so surprised that you didn't always have to live that way like you thought. We think "this is just who I am" but that is a lie. God's desire was always for us to have a transformed life to become like His Son. This is part of the sanctification process.

This is a pretty good place to talk about the third way weeds get planted in our lives, by the enemy of our souls.

Last week we discussed how we plant seeds and how others plant seeds. This week we are going to talk about how the enemy plants seeds. It's not often we talk about the enemy and how he operates. But it is very difficult to defeat what we do not understand. My hope is that after this section you would see just how the enemy operates and how to practically identify the ways in which you have unknowingly allowed him to plant seeds in your life.

The Enemy Plants Seeds

We discussed Adam and Eve and their introduction to sin and shame through the serpent. We heard about how he planted a seed of doubt in Eve's mind through the question, "Did God really say?" This is the same question we hear him telling us over and over again in different ways.

DOUBT

"Does she really want to be your friend?"

"Do they really like you?"

"Wouldn't you enjoy your life more if…?"

"Who are you to do…?"

DISCOURAGEMENT

"It will always be this way."

"I'll never be enough."

"I am not pretty enough, smart enough, capable enough."

"Bad things always happen to me."

Genesis 3:1 says *"Now the serpent was more crafty than any of the wild animals the LORD God had made."* As I looked up that word crafty in the original Hebrew it is the word *'aruwm*[6] which can be defined as "shrewd, crafty, sly, and subtle." Our Western world has created an image of the devil as a cartoon character. He appears blatantly evil and dark in every depiction we have of him, yet the Bible tells us he is subtle. He is that voice that is whispering lies of doubt and discouragement. He rejoices when we hold on to unforgiveness or pride. He is happy when we gossip about a friend or get easily offended or distracted by the shiny things of this world. He is subtle.

In the book *Screwtape Letters* by C.S. Lewis[7], the character Screwtape is having a conversation with his apprentice Wormwood. He is advising his prodigy on how to draw someone away from God and closer to Hell. I know, a light topic. If the enemy was trying to draw you away from God, what would he do or say?

The enemy is known as the accuser and the father of lies. I began to realize that I had been listening to tapes in my head that I believed to the core of who I was as truth, but they very often were lies. As I began to realize that not all of my thoughts were truth, I was shocked. Let me unpack a few of them for you.

When I got married, I moved to a new city. I didn't know anyone. I started to believe a lie that I wasn't really worth knowing and allowed a seed of low self-worth to be planted which later bloomed into a weed of depression. During this time, I befriended a woman who became a mentor figure and friend. Through a text message of some sort I shared with her that she was one of my best friends, and really one of my only friends. For me it was an act of desperation, a cry for help to say, "Be my friend!!" Which as I know now doesn't really ever go over very well. I don't think I received the response I hoped for. It was nothing negative, just not the life-long BFF I had hoped for. The reality was, I was in such a dark place I was looking for her to be my saviour. This isn't healthy on any level.

There was nothing overtly negative about this relationship, but over time I began to feel as though any invitation from her was merely because she pitied me. In my heart I believed that I wasn't good enough to be her friend and that she didn't really like me.

Over ten years went by. One day after receiving a late birthday party invitation I realized that I had a strange emotional response to her invite. (As we previously discussed - a neon sign.) It was a "Well she's just inviting me late because she doesn't really like me" sort of response. I thought for a second, "That doesn't really line up." Something inside me was confused but enlightened all at the same time. I decided that possibly perhaps I had created a story about how she saw me for all these years simply because of one text message.

I decided to do something about it. I courageously set up a coffee date. To make a long story short I shared with her the lie that I had been believing all these years and she was beyond surprised to hear this. Her shocked face was enough to confirm that this lie was just indeed that, a lie. She truly valued me and our friendship, and the season of the "text message" was one where she was actually struggling personally and she didn't even recall it.

I began to wonder how many other areas in my life I had been believing lies.

Around this same time I took a personality test where the results pointed out that I was a very social person. It stressed that I was big on friendship and that it was very important to me. But I didn't feel like I had many friends in this season of my life. I was confused. If friendships were that important to me why didn't I make more of an effort to befriend people?

I began to realize that I had been protecting myself from getting hurt by not reaching out to people, and that I had been telling myself a story about how they saw me. I had been giving their "no" for them. When I received a "sorry can't come" text after I extended an invite, I believed it was because the person didn't like me, not that they actually couldn't come.

The lies I was believing were incredibly subtle. They stole my joy. They kept me from being free to be my true self; who God created me to be.

Part of this process of digging deeper is trying to figure out where the lie came from to be able to uproot it. When we know the source, the lie is much easier to get rid of.

The Thief

> "The thief comes only to steal and kill and destroy; I have come that they may have life, and have it to the full."
>
> **JOHN 10:10**

Only recently did I discover that I am a bit of a "word nerd." I love looking at words from the Bible in their original Greek or Hebrew. I love how studying these words bring the Bible to life for me. And because I like to break it down, I'm going to pull apart this verse for you.

The thief: Greek word **kleptēs**[8] which means "an embezzler." An embezzler is someone who is dealing badly with what has been entrusted to them. But here's the thing we need to know. The enemy has no authority in our lives. None. The only authority he has is *what we give him.* Jesus is the one with all authority. Not a bit, not some, but all authority.

> "All the authority of the universe has been given to me."
>
> **MATTHEW 28:18 (TPT)**

We know the devil is a thief by nature and has zero authority. So how does he get authority? How do we give it to him? Essentially when we believe his lies. When we listen to what he is saying and partner with it instead of partnering with the truth. And because he is so crafty and subtle sometimes, he will tell us a lie that sounds like the truth. Sometimes there will even be a little bit of truth in it, but truth that is mixed with a lie is still a lie. This is why we need to be good at discerning God's voice and the truth from the lies of the enemy. Anything that produces fear, doubt, anxiety, or discouragement is straight from the enemy.

When we partner with worry, we are agreeing with the enemy that there is a reason to fear. We stop trusting that God is in control and try to take back that control for ourselves. This is how we give the enemy authority in our lives.

Let's keep breaking it down.

Steal: Greek word **kleptō**[9] which means "to steal," where we get our word kleptomaniac; the enemy is compulsively attempting to steal from us. It is constant. He wants to steal our joy, and steal our peace. In John 14:27 Jesus tells us that He gives us the gift of peace. And the enemy comes right along trying to steal it. But he can't take from us what we don't give him. The Passion Translation words it this way, *"Don't yield to fear or be troubled in your hearts."* In other words, don't give in! These are actions on our part.

Sometimes we feel like we are helpless when it comes to fear and anxiety but Jesus is asking us to be strong, don't give in.

> *"I leave the gift of peace with you—my peace. Not the kind of fragile peace given by the world, but my perfect peace. Don't yield to fear or be troubled in your hearts—instead, be courageous!"*
> **JOHN 14:27 (TPT)**

When I look at some of the root words in this verse. It is like Jesus is saying, "I'm giving you a gift. Please accept this gift. It's yours to take and yours to steward." I don't know if you've ever given someone a gift that they rejected, lost, or simply didn't use. How upset would you be? Jesus is giving us instructions here for the gift that is peace. It is nearly impossible to hold this gift of peace when our hands are busy clutching fear and anxiety.

Kill: Greek word *thyō*[10] which means "to sacrifice;" and what he can't take from us he tries to get us to sacrifice, to lay down, to give him. This word explains what I was just discussing. This is where the enemy tries to get us to sacrifice our peace and our joy, which we do when we partner with fear.

I want to pause for a second because for many of us fear seems uncontrollable. It feels like it comes upon us and we are powerless. I want to share two important thoughts about fighting fear:

1. When we have been plagued by anxiety and fear for a long time, this is going to feel like a battle. This is going to be difficult at first. It will feel like you are having to stand up to fearful and anxious thoughts pretty continuously and it may feel a bit exhausting. BUT - it is just like building any other type of muscle. When we go to the gym at first, we don't know what to do and we are pretty weak. But if we go consistently, we will begin to know what we are doing; we will gain confidence and we will get stronger!

2. The theme verse for today says *"God has not given us the spirit of fear."* 2 Timothy 1:7 Did you catch that? A spirit. Often, we are not fighting against something that is tangible but spiritual.

> *"For our struggle is not against flesh and blood, but against the rulers, against the authorities, against the powers of this dark world and against the spiritual forces of evil in the heavenly realms."*
> **EPHESIANS 6:12**

As this battle is spiritual, we need to be able to fight back using specific weapons.

> *"For although we live in the natural realm, we don't wage a military campaign employing human weapons, using manipulation to achieve our aims. Instead, our spiritual weapons are energized with divine power to effectively dismantle the defenses behind which people hide. We can demolish every deceptive fantasy that opposes God and break through every arrogant attitude that is raised up in defiance of the true knowledge of God. We capture, like prisoners of war, every thought and insist that it bow in obedience to the Anointed One."*
> **2 CORINTHIANS 10:4-5 (TPT)**

I love the way The Passion Translation describes this process, *"We capture, like prisoners of war."* This is not us sitting passively on the sidelines, this is us on the front lines, being active. If we were in a battle on the ground and found an enemy in our camp, we would do our best to wrestle that enemy into our control and take them captive. It is the same with our thought life. For many of us we simply have been a little too relaxed about what we have allowed our minds to dwell on and what we have allowed to enter in. Before I move on to the word destroy from John 10:10 I want to share a story that highlights this point.

Brendan was out for the night and the girls and I went down to the basement to play for a bit before bed. When I went downstairs, I noticed the back door was unlocked. Immediately I had this thought, "Someone may have come in and is hiding in the basement." Now logically, I knew why the door was unlocked. Brendan had been schlepping stuff from the basement, up the back steps, to the garage all afternoon and we simply didn't lock it again. But even though I had a logical, rational, answer; I let fear take over.

Fear doesn't operate in logic and it doesn't operate in the rational.

Rather than taking that thought captive - stopping it at the door of my heart and head - I fed it by opening every cupboard and closet in the basement (in the safety of the presence of my children). And even though my search came up empty, I had allowed fear in. In doing so I gave the enemy authority to grow that seed of fear into a weed of anxiety.

I put the kids to bed and tried to go to sleep myself. I could tell I was feeling anxious and that often resulted in my adrenaline pumping and sleep being a long way off - if it would come at all. I painstakingly waited until Brendan's ETA of 11:00 pm came and went and then sent a very calm text around 11:09 pm. "Hey, just wondering when you're home…" (He was at a late-night board game party with some friends).

As I awaited his response, I allowed that weed of fear to take me on an emotional roller coaster ride. I quickly went from sending an inquiring text about arrival time to imagining the worst had occurred. In my mind, I was suddenly a widow; "Wait is that why I was feeling anxious earlier? Is God preparing me to be a widow? Will I marry again? Do I want to marry again? Will anyone want to marry me? Does this mean I need to start working out? Wait - I don't want to marry anyone else, no one else can deal with all of my weird quirks like Brendan." ALL of these thoughts and more came flooding in a 30 second span and I was on the verge of actual real life tears, planning a funeral and a wedding all at the same time.

Ding! There's the text message, his party ran late and he was on his way home. Right. Not a widow. I had allowed fear to have authority and take over my heart and my mind. I felt a physical reaction and was living my thoughts as if they were actually happening. Remember what I said earlier about emotions being masters?

My emotion of fear could have been used to point to the root of the issue, instead I let it run wild and I opened the door for fear to have authority in my life.

I wish this was a one-time experience. But this had happened far too often and I was sick of it. What I didn't realize then but know now is that fear doesn't have to rule. However, I have to have the discipline and self-control to check it at the door. I can't entertain it. I can't allow that seed to get planted. And for me, that night, I opened the door to fear when I had the thought of someone entering my home in the basement. That was the moment I let fear in. Rather than checking it at the door - I let it in and let it run wild. What I should have done is capture that thought like a prisoner of war. As I mentioned earlier, if you are not used to capturing your thoughts it may feel like a lot of work, and it may feel like you are having to take captive thoughts every 30 seconds. But it does get easier. When we begin to practice guarding our minds, we will become stronger and more skilled at deflecting the lies of the enemy.

To finish off our study of John 10:10 I want to look at the word destroy.

Destroy: Greek word apollymi11 - there are a few good definitions here, "to put out of the way entirely" and "render useless" are my favourite. They paint such a good picture of what the enemy tries to do to us. He wants to get us and the great things God has put inside us out of the way. He wants to render us useless. I have seen this many times in my life when I am lying in a heap on the couch totally hopeless and helpless. Or when I find myself paralyzed, not really sure what I should be doing with my time.

When I find myself in that state, I try to ask myself the question, "If I were the enemy what three things would I be doing to take Jaclyn out right now?" Sometimes it helps to know who it is we are fighting against. We often think it is our spouse or our kids, or our in-laws. But often, when we realize that those people are not our enemy, the tension dissipates and the real issue can be dealt with. We have a real enemy and he is trying to render us useless.

We read in this week's theme verse that God won't give us the spirit of fear. So, if we sense the spirit of fear - we know it is from the enemy. He will bring that spirit of fear any way that is effective against you. If it has worked once he will try it again. He is not a creator, he is not God. He is sly as we saw above. If something worked on you before he will come again and again with that same tactic. And if you experience freedom in one area of your life, he will try to bring up shame in another.

The enemy loves to operate in fear. When we fear we are paralyzed; remember "destroy" or render useless. I am useless when I am paralyzed by fear. He comes in and paralyzes me by fear and steals my joy. And I give it over. I sacrifice it.

How does he do this?

One of the ways he does this is by tricking us into believing that he is big. But he is not. He is small. He is not omnipotent; he is not omnipresent. But he has a bag of tricks and uses whatever works on us. As we begin to identify the truth from the lies, and as we practice taking our thoughts captive we won't be as easily tricked into becoming paralyzed.

I remember when I realized I no longer feared going down to the basement or to dark places by myself. It wasn't that long ago. But I realized, "Hey, I'm not afraid anymore!" Like Macaulay Culkin in *Home Alone*[12] when he shouts outside the front of his house at the burglars, "I'm not afraid anymore!"

Because when you are able to find freedom from fear you want to shout it from the rooftops!

The second half of John 10:10 says *"I have come that they may have life, and have it to the full."* And in The Passion Translation, *"But I have come to give you everything in abundance, more than you expect - life in its fullness until you overflow!"*

THAT is worth shouting about.

When the weed of fear is removed from the garden of our soul, we will feel a lightness and a freedom that will be palpable to everyone around us. Many in the world are walking around in an invisible bondage to fear. We may not realize it as we often learn to cope with the things that cause anxiety in our lives. Often the people we hang out with experience similar fears so we begin to think they are "normal." But this is simply another way of ensuring this weed gets stuck in our garden. We think to ourselves, "Everyone else is experiencing the same thing." It is only when we taste true freedom that we realize just how chained up we were.

As I mentioned before, the lies that leave us in bondage can be subtle. Some of my lies have included "People will like me more if I dress plainly, I should try not to shine." "My friends don't really like me; they just feel sorry for me." "I am not smart enough, or good enough." "My past has disqualified me for God to do anything of value with my life." "You were born this way; this is part of your DNA." "Things will always be this way."

I recently had the opportunity to go to a small women's retreat. We had the chance to sit quietly and think about the lies swirling around in our minds. And even though we know them to be lies, we believe them to our core. As I sat in the circle and listened to the other women share the lies they believed about themselves it took everything in me to not jump up and shout "That is not true! It is a lie!" It was so obvious to me and others around me that those things each woman believed about herself was a lie. But when a lie is so deeply rooted it is more difficult to identify and uproot.

Sometimes we need a friend to sit with us and speak the truth into our lives. And always, we need to sit quietly with God and allow His truth-whispers to identify the lie and cover it with His truth. When we allow God's words of love to wash over us, it loosens the grip of the lies in our heart and even begins to uproot them for us.

SONG: "You Say" by Lauren Daigle[13]

DISCUSSION QUESTIONS:

1) Have you ever had an overly emotional response to a situation?
   Looking back did you choose to fight or flight?
   Do you think there was a deeper root to the issue?

2) Are you struggling with a seed of doubt or discouragement? Can you think about where it may have come from?

3) Is there an area in your life where you are experiencing fear?

4) What lies do you believe about yourself? (Allow others to speak truth here).

Digging Deeper - Set aside time to be still before God and talk together about your heart soil.

1) Pull out your calendar and plan a 1-2 hour window where you can have this quiet time. Right now, decide on where that will be, come up with an outdoor and an indoor option where you can be totally alone. You will need your Bible, this book and possibly a journal and some worship music. I like music to help prepare my heart to hear from God but don't be afraid to just sit in the silence of the moment. Yes, this is what I said last week!

2) Sometimes digging deeper means getting help to get to the root of the issue. This is going to be HARD for some of you. Find a true, trusted friend and ask them to help you. Share with them the lies you are believing and allow them to speak truth over you. Pray together to release these lies and declare the love and truth of Jesus into the places they took up space in your head and heart.

"For where two or three gather in my name, there am I with them."
MATTHEW 18:20

3) Lies vs Truth exercise: This is NOT easy to do but it is such a life-changing exercise. Write down any lie you hear regularly. Anything such as "I am not enough." Anything that causes fear, anxiety, discontent is from the enemy. Write down a truth beside that statement even if you have trouble "feeling" that it is true. Spend a bit of time praying and see if any truth found in scripture goes with your truth. Write that down. These are your life verses. These are tools to be used against the lies of the enemy. Memorize these and declare them out loud over yourself.

LIES	TRUTH

4) Look up 2 Corinthians 10:5 in at least three different translations and write down the one that resonated most with you.

WEEK 3

Uprooting

I am so excited for this week! We have spent the last two weeks talking about what weeds are and how we identify them in our lives. Now is the fun part! We get to talk about how to get rid of the weeds in our life. Well maybe not "fun" but this is where real transformation will take place!

First let's talk about what keeps the weeds locked in the soil of our heart. Weeds thrive in the dark; metaphorically anyways. We keep secrets locked away in our heart as a means of self-preservation and protection. We believe if our deep soul sins were brought out into the light we would not be able to handle the shame and embarrassment. Like Adam and Eve, we instinctively hide away when we have sinned and hide our sin away in our hearts. Maybe there would be painful consequences if we brought things into the light? So, we sit on them. We bury things deep within our heart that we do not want anyone to know about. We believe that is the safest way to protect ourselves. Little do we realize we are building our own chains in that process.

VERSE OF THE WEEK

"God did not send his Son into the world to judge and condemn the world, but to be its Saviour and rescue it!"
JOHN 3:17 (TPT)

Condemnation vs Conviction

Sometimes when we sit with the Gardener of our soul, and something we need to deal with is brought to the forefront of our mind we feel something called conviction. Conviction is different than condemnation. Condemnation is a trick used by the enemy to wrap what we have done in the past in shame. As I shared last week, shame is not from God. The enemy brought shame into the Garden of Eden and he is the one who brings it into the garden of our hearts.

This is where many of us get stuck. We are afraid of feeling condemned by our past actions and feel shame about what we have done. So, we don't do anything about it. We sit in that pain and shame allowing ourselves to be destroyed from the inside out.

But we know Jesus destroyed sin AND shame on the cross. Our theme verse for the week tells us *"God did not send his Son into the world to judge and condemn the world, but to be its Saviour and rescue it!"* John 3:17 (TPT)

This process of removing weeds in our life is for our freedom - and the price has already been paid. We just need to let go of the things that are holding us hostage. Let's talk about how we can practically do that.

Confession and Repentance

It is confession that cuts the cords of the sin that so easily entangles.

If this is new to you it can seem backwards and scary. Especially if you are a private person and are not comfortable sharing much at all with others. The idea of confession can be terrifying. Let me first calm your heart by sharing that our main confession is to God alone. In Psalm 51 David confesses and repents of his sin with Bathsheba and prays "against you, you only, have I sinned" (vs 4). David's example of confession and repentance is that whatever we may have done it is God's forgiveness we are seeking.

In that same Psalm, David shows us the act of true repentance and what God is really after through our confession. *"My sacrifice, O God, is a broken spirit; a broken and contrite heart, you, God, will not despise,"* (vs 17). It's not about reciting a line or a series of steps to follow, it is about our heart posture. It is always about our heart posture. The thing I love about David is that he screwed up. He was human, as human as you and I. Despite committing adultery and murder he was written about as a man after God's own heart. Not because he was so great, but because of his heart posture.

I think that's ultimately what God wants from us, not perfection. We don't have it in us, we are human. Let's get over trying to be perfect. Let's let go of trying to attain something in our own strength that will ultimately lead to our destruction. Let's instead realize we are dust, jars of clay, made weak and breakable to showcase His strength in and through us. Let us rejoice in our weakness because His *"power is made perfect in weakness."* 2 Corinthians 12:9

Ultimately Christ is the one that will do the weeding in our lives. But we are active participants, it is not a passive process. Confession and repentance are the active ways in which we are able to release the grip that weeds have in our lives. Through our verbal declaration, we are able to let go of weeds that may have been holding onto us even before we were born.

As you begin to confess and repent of the weeds in your life, hand them over to Jesus to do the major uprooting. Pray these things out loud. Break agreement with any weed that comes to mind. There is power in the name of Jesus. He has given you authority in your life through His name to pray against any stronghold that may have a hold in your life. Declare this stronghold must be broken in Jesus' name. Confession and repentance weakens this attachment allowing the grip to be loosened and praying in authority is the final tug to free your heart from this weed. As you pray these weeds out of your heart and your life you may feel a physical lightness. This is your garden being freed from weeds.

Once you have finished praying for weeds to be uprooted pray a prayer of blessing over yourself. Ask that the Holy Spirit would fill in all the places those weeds left. The enemy does not like you praying in authority or removing strongholds from your life. He will try to fill your mind with doubt that nothing really happened, that you're not really free.

It is important to be aware of those thoughts when they come and take captive every thought and make it obedient to Christ. Do not entertain those thoughts and plant seeds of doubt. It is much easier to deal with a weed when it is on the surface before it has been planted, so don't allow new weeds to get planted. This is where it is so important to know the difference between the voice of God and the voice of the enemy.

The thoughts of the enemy produce doubt, fear, and anxiety.
The voice of God will produce love, peace, and hope.

Like any garden you won't necessarily uproot all of the weeds at one time. Sometimes uprooting one weed will reveal another. Sometimes a weed is really big and strong and requires some help in removal. And that is okay too. You may need to have a friend or a few trusted friends join you in the process. Where two or more are gathered God is there. (Matthew 18:20)

The other thing about weed removal is that it helps to be specific. Praying vague prayers like "I confess I didn't act the way I should have" is not helpful. Specifically praying "I confess that I had lustful thoughts about John," or "I confess I am bitter and unforgiving towards Sarah," is much more effective in releasing the stronghold of the weed.

What happens when we do all of this work, all of this confession and repentance and yet it still feels like we have more weeding to do? Don't be discouraged, weeding is a lifelong process. But once we do the hard work of removing the biggest weeds it becomes more about strengthening and maintaining than heavy weed removal.

Sometimes it feels like we've done a bunch of weeding through confession and repentance but there still seems to be some big weeds that don't want to go. This may be for a few reasons. One, we may have lived with some of these weeds for a long time and the enemy does not want to release the stronghold he's had on our lives. Two, there may be other things keeping those weeds locked in place. Unforgiveness is a big one.

Forgiveness

By not forgiving someone we remain attached to that painful experience in our lives. That is part of the tangling.

> *"For if you forgive other people when they sin against you, your heavenly Father will also forgive you. But if you do not forgive others their sins, your Father will not forgive your sins."*
> **MATTHEW 6:14-15**

These are the words of Jesus during His famous Sermon on the Mount. These words come right after He teaches the disciples (and us) how to pray. Inside this well-known Lord's Prayer there is a call to action on our part towards forgiveness.

> *"Forgive us our debts, as we also have forgiven our debtors."*
> **MATTHEW 6:12**

The Bible discusses forgiveness countless times and for years I brushed it off as yet another thing I needed "to do" as a Christian. Like so many other things I was unaware that this was not an act for me to do but to receive. As I forgive others their debts I experience freedom. Freedom in my heart from the offence they have caused me.

This offence may range from someone cutting you off while driving, a friend speaking unkindly to you or worse behind your back, or someone who has physically or verbally abused you. We seem to have an internal ranking system when it comes to offence, but there is no rating system when it comes to forgiveness, or unforgiveness.

Please don't get me wrong, I am in no way saying that a rude driver is in the same category as someone assaulting you. However, where so many of us get stuck is waiting for an apology that will never come. Holding on to the offence that occurred, no matter how wrong it was, no matter how justified the unforgiveness, it simply keeps those weeds of hurt and pain locked inside the soil of our heart.

I am not an expert on pain, or an expert on forgiveness, but I know that this is a place where so many of us have yet to experience freedom. We hold on to things that are absolutely justified because we don't want the other party to win.

> *We don't want our forgiveness to somehow make what they did ok.*

It wasn't and it's not, but by forgiving the other person we are engaging in an <u>act of freedom</u>. We are saying what you did no longer has a hold on me or power over me. In the words of Christine Caine who was herself physically abused for 12 years "I've made what Jesus did *for* me bigger than what anyone did *to* me."[14]

Again, not an expert, and I can't say this will be quick, or easy. But it is necessary, for our compete freedom. If you would like an expert opinion on why this is important, Dr. Caroline Leaf a cognitive neuroscientist explains that "When you forgive, you disentangle yourself from that situation." "By forgiving you're actually disconnecting from the toxicity of that situation." There is a physiological response when we forgive others. (Dr Caroline Leaf Podcast Episode #54)[15]

Sometimes there is one big thing we are holding onto that is keeping us from walking in freedom. Other times it is many little things added together, "death by 1,000 cuts." For some of us it is the little offences that are keeping us from our freedom. It is the family member who knows how to push our buttons, it is the friend that has disappointed us, it is the server in a bad mood that took it out on us. It doesn't really matter what it is, the result is the same. We focus more on what was done to us and how we have been hurt, wronged, and offended.

And then we ensure we stay in that place through our own actions of complaining, gossiping, and slandering. Here's the rub. Here's the hard part. You likely haven't done anything wrong. You likely are in the "right." So, you "have every right" to complain. You have every right to be frustrated with that person and their actions. BUT here is what it does to you.

It keeps you stuck. It keeps you from living light and free.

We will talk more about this in Week 6 but it's helpful to touch on it now as a means of uprooting the weeds in our heart. Sometimes there is one huge deeply rooted weed, and other times it is a sea of similar weeds that seem to require a lot of attention.

Do not be discouraged. Although weeding is not a "one and done" process as we would like, once we are able to identify the ways in which weeds have been planted, we can stop them before they begin the next time and we have less regular weeding to attend to.

We have discussed confession and repentance as our primary method of uprooting weeds. I want to share about another method, using the Sword of the Spirit.

The Sword of the Spirit

In Ephesians 6 Paul writes about the Armour of God. He describes various pieces of "armour" to wear and how they will protect us from the flaming arrows of the evil one. Throughout this armour there is only one that is an offensive piece, the Sword of the Spirit.

When I would read this chunk of Scripture, I was always so confused about how to use this sword. "Wait, do I just wave my Bible around? Do I sleep with it under my pillow? How do I use my sword? How is the Bible to be used as a weapon against the enemy?"

First off, the word sword here in Greek is **machaira**[16] and it refers to "a large knife or a small sword." It was used for "thrusting." This is the type of sword that was used in battle to kill an opponent, with a quick, swift stab. This was not a sword intended for a 'sword fight' as we might imagine, as in the epic battle in the Princess Bride between Inigo Montoya and the Man In Black.[17] We are not meant to duel our enemy but to defeat him. And we are to use the Word of God.

> *"The sword of the Spirit, which is the word of God."*
> **EPHESIANS 6:17**

The Greek word here for "word" is not the word **logos** which is often used to refer to the entirety of the Bible but rather the word **rhēma**[18], which means "that which is or has been uttered, a thing spoken, or speech." It is the spoken Word of God. God wants us to use His spoken Word to defeat our enemy.

Jesus showed us this example while He was being tempted in the desert. The enemy came at Him three times and each time He defeated him through Scripture, through the spoken Word of God.

> *"The tempter came to him and said, "If you are the Son of God, tell these stones to become bread." Jesus answered, "It is written: 'Man shall not live on bread alone, but on every word that comes from the mouth of God.'"*
> **MATTHEW 4:3-4**

Notice how devil didn't just try random things to attack Jesus? The enemy knew where His pain point was. He was hungry. He hadn't eaten in 40 days. Jesus was fully human. This was not a joke to Him. He possessed the ability to turn the stones to bread. This was actually not a ridiculous thing for the enemy to say. It seemed like a pretty good idea in many ways. Jesus had a need and the enemy tried to provide an answer.

Doesn't that happen in our own lives as well? We have a need. A legitimate need. And the enemy comes along with a legitimate answer. Maybe our need is for connection. We try and fill that need. It doesn't always seem "bad" or "wrong." That's the tricky thing with weeds. They aren't all bad on the surface. *It's when we turn to these things to fill our needs instead of turning to God.* He alone is able to satisfy all of our needs. We often turn to every other thing first. We are human, looking for a human answer.

We need to follow Jesus' model when it comes to defeating this very real enemy that comes after us when we are in the wilderness. Notice the enemy didn't take Jesus to the wilderness, the Spirit led Him there (vs 4:1). Sometimes God is taking us through a wilderness to grow us. Maybe you find yourself there now. What will happen in this wilderness? Will you give in to the temptation of the enemy or will you grow into maturity by making the hard decision to choose God each and every time temptation comes your way?

Jesus spoke out loud the written Word of God and this was what defeated His enemy. The same is true for us today. And this is why it's so important to be reading the Word of God. We need to plant the Word in our heart so when the time comes, the Holy Spirit will give us the words to say just as He promised.

> *"But the Advocate, the Holy Spirit, whom the Father will send in my name, will teach you all things and will remind you of everything I have said to you."*
>
> **JOHN 14:26**

We don't need to worry about memorizing everything, every passage, and where it is found. If we really need to know, Google can help with that! But we need to be planting the Word in our heart and the Holy Spirit will bring to mind scriptures to defeat the enemy.

When I face the "temptation" of fear, am I going to give into that temptation to be afraid or choose to trust God? Think back to 2 Timothy 1:7, *"For God will never give you the spirit of fear, but the Holy Spirit who gives you mighty power, love, and self-control." (TPT)*

This won't necessarily be easy to do or come naturally at first, but as we learn our **rhēma** words it will get easier. It is like building muscle. The first time we work out a new part of our body it is hard. But the more we choose this action it becomes more second nature and we will be able to do it more easily.

I had an experience recently where I felt like I was not connected to God. I don't believe He went anywhere but I think He wanted me to learn the power of **rhēma** words to break strongholds. I was slotted to speak briefly at a local women's conference and as with other times in my life where I am stepping out in a bigger way and sharing my faith, I can often feel like the enemy tries to press in harder.

The week leading up to the conference I was just feeling "off." I can't say that it was all heavy spiritual warfare but I knew the first night of the conference that something wasn't right. I felt a bit disconnected to God. I did all of the things I knew to do, I used all of the tools in my tool belt but it still seemed like something wasn't right. I knew I needed to wake up extra early the morning of my talk to have some time being quiet with God and make sure my head and heart were in the right place. I was so frustrated as I began to get ready, "Why wasn't I feeling connected to God?" He brought to mind the idea of **rhēma** words. I thought for a minute, "But God what words do YOU want me to say?" Not in a formulaic way, but I just wondered what words would be effective. He gently reminded me that He had been giving me a verse for a month and a half.

I spoke this verse out loud. And as I spoke it, something inside me broke. I felt it physically lift and I was in tears. I felt His presence. "Ahh" I thought, "This is the power of **rhēma** words." And God wanted me to know the power of having this tool in my tool belt.

I believe He will give us the words to use in our time of need. There is power in using the Sword of the Spirit to defeat our enemy and cut these weeds out of our life.

The last tool for uprooting weeds in our soul sounds very simple but is incredibly powerful and biblical. Praise. All throughout Scripture we are called to praise.

Worship as Warfare

"Praise the LORD, my soul; all my inmost being, praise his holy name."
PSALM 103:1

"The Lord is my strength and my song, and he has become my salvation; this is my God, and I will praise him, my father's God, and I will exalt him.
EXODUS 15:2 (ESV)

"Yet I will rejoice in the Lord, I will be joyful in God my Savior."
HABAKKUK 3:18

Throughout the Bible, songs are written and sung by Moses, Mary, Hannah and David as remembrance of what God has done in their lives. The way He has fulfilled promises, the way He has come through. There is power in praise.

This is evident in Acts 16 where we see Paul and Silas have been beaten and thrown into prison after healing a woman from the evil spirit that was inside her. It's sort of a funny story as this woman was following them around and it basically says Paul told this spirit to leave because he was just so annoyed. I like to imagine him turning and having compassion on her, but this was not the case. *"Finally Paul became so annoyed that he turned around and said to the spirit, "In the name of Jesus Christ I command you to come out of her!" At that moment the spirit left her." Acts 16:18*

But she was a slave, and this act of freedom meant her owners would no longer be able to make money through the spirit that had inhabited her. As a result, Paul and Silas were thrown in prison.

If I were them, this is what our conversation may have looked like. (As Silas) "Way to go Paul, you let your temper get in the way again and now we're going to die here. Why did I ever agree to come with you?" (Keep in mind, Silas wasn't even originally going on this trip, it was supposed to be Paul and Barnabas but they got in a fight and split ways! Silas was second choice!) Maybe Paul was still fuming from his fight with Barnabas and just generally annoyed with this new city, annoyed that he had his number two guy...

We don't really know where their heads were at or what they were thinking. We do know that they were unfairly thrown in prison and had received a terrible beating. I think at that moment, I may have just thought, "Maybe it would be better to die. This is hard, too hard. I did my best, I followed what God said and now here I am."

Either of those two scenarios are realistic. Blaming someone else for getting you in this predicament, or just wanting to die in it. Likely if they had chosen either of those two scenarios they would have died right there in that prison.

But they chose door number three, and with God there is always a third option if we are willing to look to Him.

> *"About midnight Paul and Silas were praying and singing hymns to God, and the other prisoners were listening to them. Suddenly there was a violent earthquake that the foundations of the prison were shaken. At once all the prison doors flew open, and everyone's chains came loose."*
> **ACTS 16:25-26**

They were in pain. They may have thought they were going to die or even wanted to die. It wasn't their "fault" they were in prison. But they didn't focus on any of those things.

Sometimes we just need to praise our way out of a situation.

They were praying and singing hymns to God. Other versions say "Sang songs of praise," and "Singing a robust hymn." (TPT and The Message) They weren't just half-heartedly singing; they were singing like they meant it. They weren't sitting in a pity party, or blaming anyone else for their circumstances. They weren't complaining about the pain of their beating. Or trying to figure out how they were possibly going to get out of their situation. They instead chose to praise, and that is what broke their chains! Not only did it break *their* chains but it broke the chains of others.

Other people are watching us in our pain. They are looking to see how we respond to the little struggles of life and to the major crises we walk through. It's not that we need to drum up some special strength in our own selves and "fake it till we make it" because this is what a good Christian does or looks like. But we are to walk through our pain with Him, and then choose to not wallow in self-pity or blame but instead to choose praise. It is a choice. It is one of the ways we will experience freedom from the chains that entangle.

Our freedom is never just for ourselves. As we share the powerful stories of the transformation we experience through Christ, others will be set free as well. In the same way the chains of the other prisoners came loose when Paul and Silas were liberated; others will experienced freedom as we share our stories.

> *"They triumphed over him by the blood of the Lamb and by the word of their testimony."*
> **REVELATION 12:11**

Our verse of the week says, *"God did not send his Son into the world to judge and condemn the world, but to be its Saviour and rescue it!"* John 3:17 (TPT) And this is ultimately where we receive our freedom. Not through any of the actions I've discussed on our own, but because Jesus died. He paid the price for our freedom and He longs for us to walk in it. Like really walk in freedom. Regardless of our past, regardless of our current life circumstances or all that will come to us. We receive our freedom through His death and resurrection, not because of anything we have done, can or will do.

> *"It is for freedom that Christ has set us free. Stand firm, then, and do not let yourselves be burdened again by a yoke of slavery."*
> **GALATIANS 5:1**

SONG: *"Defender"* by Rita Springer[19]

DISCUSSION QUESTIONS:

1) Where do you sometimes get stuck in the forgiveness process?

2) Have you ever had a conversation in your head with someone where you try and convince them of your point/side of the story? How are you left feeling afterwards in general and towards the other person?

3) What does the term "sacrifice of praise" mean to you?

LIFEWORK:

1) Are there weeds that still need uprooting? Ask the Holy Spirit to reveal the weeds you need to uproot and give them over to God. Psalm 46:10 says *"Be still, and know that I am God."* The phrase "be still" in Hebrew is the word *raphah*[20] which means "to sink down, relax, let drop, to let go." While you sit and be still allow your hands to loosen; to relax. Allow yourself to let go of your worries and fears. Open your hands and your heart in a posture of surrender to Him as you, together, take part in this uprooting process.

The word "know" in Hebrew is the word *yada'*[21] which is "to know, perceive, admit, acknowledge, confess, to be known." Enter into a heart posture where you "know" that He is God. Use this time to walk through the steps of confession and repentance as previously discussed.

2) The process of forgiveness can be difficult, especially depending on the severity of the offence. Is there anyone you need to forgive? If we don't acknowledge the actions done to us, they can begin to destroy us from the inside out. Denying anything done wrong can keep us from being able to forgive and let go properly. We may need to freak out a little bit, either to God or to a safe friend. We may need a time we can yell, cry, say "All the things" and really get it off our chest. We need to release all of the pain we have been holding onto. Once we've let it all out we can begin the process of forgiving.

This is an optional but effective exercise: write them a letter. Tell them all of the ways in which they hurt you. Don't leave anything out and be specific. Hold that letter in front of you and talk to God about it. What does He want to say about the situation? Ask Him where He was during this time. Ask Him to help you let go of this person and the unforgiveness you hold towards them. Tell God you know this doesn't make it alright, He already knows that too, but that you don't want this to have any place in your heart anymore. Give this letter to God and ask Him to fill you with love and forgiveness in places that may have held bitterness and pain. Ask Him to fill in all of the cracks. Then take the letter and destroy it, (in a safe way). This is a physical act to mirror what has been done spiritually. As you destroy the letter you are declaring a release of all ties of bitterness, unforgiveness and anything else that has a hold on you. Thank God for filling those places and choose to live in complete freedom. (As I mentioned earlier - pursuing professional counselling is encouraged.)

3) List the temptations you face regularly and ask the Holy Spirit if any Scriptures come to mind. If not, Google verses connected to this temptation. Example: temptation to control, temptation of fear, temptation of doubt, temptation to worry. Write out these verses.

4) Create a praise playlist. Look up songs on YouTube, ask friends for their favourites, find some old classics, hymns or ones you used to sing at summer camp. Create a playlist you can have as a go-to for times of prayer, when you feel like it, but especially when you don't. There is something incredibly powerful about facing a difficult situation in a posture of praise.

planting

Confession: I really, truly, honest-to-goodness believed the "fruits" of the Spirit were unattainable. Where does this mythical person exist who contains this good fruit? Have I ever met such a person? I most certainly am not a person that exudes these characteristics. Growing up I remember telling people "I am not sweet." I believed that kind people were librarians that wore cardigans and sensible shoes and I was a sarcastic person who preferred ripped jeans and a t-shirt.

It didn't take long in motherhood to have any shred of the fruit of the Spirit ripped from my vision of attainability. It seemed not a day or even sometimes an hour would go by that I didn't lose my patience. (Of course, losing it indicates that I had any patience at all to begin with.) I've come to appreciate this about marriage and motherhood. You can't hide behind a facade to your spouse the way you can from other people. You can't present a fake representation of yourself to your kids. You can try but you will eventually reveal your true self.

Living in close community with others has a way of exposing your flaws like no other. Whether living with roommates, a husband, or your children. When those things are uncovered we have a few options: we can deny what we are feeling/what is being revealed, we can feel hopeless, like this is how I will always be, or, we can dig in and lean into what has come to the surface.

You see, here's the thing with our "flaws," or those things that come to the surface, whatever you want to call them. Having them come up is a really good thing. Remember, the purpose of refining is to purify. Precious stones are refined to be even more valuable. The refining process is often difficult and painful, but done well it reveals the beauty that was there all along.

And that is what happens in our weeding process. Weeds are removed that are choking out the things we want in life, the good things, the beautiful things.

VERSE OF THE WEEK

"But the fruit of the spirit is love, joy, peace, patience, kindness, goodness, faithfulness, gentleness, self-control; against such things there is no law."
GALATIANS 5:22 (ESV)

Removing the Weeds
Reveals the Fruit

As we talk about planting good things in our life don't be surprised if many of them simply begin to spring up as weeds are removed. Often that is all that is needed in some areas of our lives. We let go of a weed, give it over to the Gardener for removal, and the things we want to grow will begin to sprout up.

I had an experience recently where I got into an argument with my husband. We began to fight about something that was insignificant. And isn't that often how it goes? We fight about silly things and little things and try to resolve those things without actually getting to the root of the issue.

And if we don't fully deal with the root we will continue to fight on and on about things that are actually trying to direct us to the real issue.

I sat with my husband in the car and asked him, "What do you think the real problem is here?" (We've been around the block enough to know when the things we are fighting about are not really the things we are fighting about.) "I can't really put my finger on it," was his response. It took us some time, some tears, and some open, honest, words about how we actually felt about each other regarding this issue.

The one thing I always say is the key to my marriage being strong is that we fight well. We don't just leave an issue unresolved; we dig at it and we deal with it.

We identified the root (it was a big one) and we resolved it. But as we parted ways that morning onto our separate busy plans for the day, I knew that I wasn't quite done. My husband and I felt more connected and had identified our issue. But I knew there was more that God wanted to do in my heart. So, I decided to re-arrange my schedule and drove to a nearby park along a river. It was mostly secluded and I was able to just sit and be. I sat with God and asked Him a few questions. Why was I feeling this way? Why did I respond to this issue in the way I did?

When we sit and ask God questions and allow ourselves to linger, He is so faithful to respond.

He highlighted to me that I had been operating out of fear instead of love. The surface issue was regarding my husband's very full ministry schedule. But the root issue was a deep fear that if I fully supported him, I wouldn't have enough. Enough time - for myself, with him and our family, and enough energy for our kids and many other things. It was a scarcity mindset.

We had been in an unhealthy place many years before and even though we weren't there now and hadn't been there in a long time, I allowed that fear to creep in. My fear had produced control. I began to control whatever I could to make sure we would have enough. I wanted to provide for us. Now, of course we want to be healthy and balanced and all of those good things. But here's the thing, we were generally operating well in life. I, however, was still holding onto the fear that things would go back to the way they had been before. So, I held back. I couldn't fully support him out of fear of lack.

Because God was able to highlight these things to me, I could then partner with Him by confessing my fear and the way I had been trying to control my husband and the situation. And then the most interesting thing happened.

As He took away all of the fear and control that I handed over, I began to smile. I could feel joy bubbling up in my heart. It wasn't like a "now I'm going to have a dance party" sort of joy, but a small little sprout just waiting to be cultivated. Often this is what happens.

When we allow ourselves to surrender to the pruning God wants to do in our hearts, good things are able to flourish that have otherwise been choked out.

There will always be areas in my life that need refining. I am not perfect, just ask my family! (Actually don't!) Allowing God to identify and cut away the lies, the wrong mindsets, the attitudes and anything else that is preventing me from fully thriving has been the most life-giving process.

It can almost feel like there is a clogged drain in our hearts, and once those things are removed - life - real life - can begin to flow through.

Be Intentional

I want to move on a bit from the weeding process to the planting process. What else can we do to intentionally plant good seeds? Let's get incredibly practical for a minute. Take a step back and look at what you are currently putting into the soil of your heart. Essentially, this is how you spend your waking hours. The conversations you have, the shows you watch, and the music you listen to. I think it's only appropriate that social media is termed a "newsfeed" as it is what many of us are "consuming" the most.

Whether you realize it or not, these are the seeds you are planting in your life.

Can I really expect seeds of peace when I watch a TV show starring women who scream at each other? Or when I read comments of people arguing on social media?

Can I expect seeds of self-control when I surround myself with others who are drinking heavily, or I watch a steamy movie with sexually explicit scenes?

Can I expect seeds of joy when I spend my time complaining or cultivating bitterness or offence?

Please keep in mind this has nothing to do with legalism. This is not that. This is simply being aware that what you are feeding your soul is going to produce fruit. It just may not be the fruit you want.

If you don't like the fruit you need to change the seed.

So, where do we start? When I first started planting my own garden, I didn't know anything about seeds, mulch, or fertilizer. I didn't know how long it would take to go from seed to flower or how often I would need to water or prune. The same is true for our soul life, if we haven't paid much attention to how we plant things into the soil of our heart we can't be expected to just "get it" right away. But just like in classic gardening, there are a few simple principles we can follow.

Time

Let's take a moment and take stock of how we spend our waking hours:

On your iPhone: Go to Settings - then Battery then scroll down to see usage percent and click to see actual hours spent in the last 24 hours or 10 days. These numbers don't lie. If you don't have an iPhone there are other apps where you can track and see where your time spent on technology is really going. Write down these numbers.

On your calendar: How have you structured your time? Let's take a few minutes to evaluate. Write down approximately how much time you are spending each week on activities that are "mindless" (scrolling etc.) and activities that aren't serving you well.

Spend a few minutes answering these questions for yourself:

1) Did any of these findings surprise you? If so, which area and why?

2) Is there one area you would like to spend less time or eliminate altogether?

3) If you added up the amount of time you have spent on "mindless" activities in one week what would you have time to do? What would you want to do?

I recently realized I was feeling overwhelmed by all I had to get accomplished in my week. I then paused to see how much time I had spent on mindless activities (on my phone!) over the last week. Eliminating those would give me more than enough time to accomplish what I needed to do. I just didn't have time to zone out on all of the things I was in the habit of doing.

Here's the universal truth about time. We all have the same amount. In different season of life with work, school, and family we have different amounts of "free" time at our disposal. But - for the most part we each have 168 hours in a week. We have the things we have to do, such as sleep, work, eat, and other individual responsibilities. But any remaining time is "free."

As a mom of three young kids I understand it doesn't always "feel" like I have a ton of free time. But I do have pockets, small windows of time. What I choose to do with that time will affect me. It will plant seeds in my life that will grow into fruit - even if I don't see the evidence of that fruit right away. Just like the seeds in my garden, it takes time for things to grow, and I want to be planting good seeds.

Plant the Word

I love how the first part of Isaiah 55 describes what we've already been talking about.

> "Hey there! All who are thirsty, come to the water! Are you penniless? Come anyway - buy and eat! Come, buy your drinks, buy wine and milk. Buy without money - everything's free! Why do you spend your money on junk food, your hard-earned cash on cotton candy? Listen to me, listen well: Eat only the best, fill yourself with only the finest. Pay attention, come close now, listen carefully to my life-giving, life-nourishing words."
>
> ISAIAH 55:1-3 (THE MESSAGE)

This is a beautiful picture of the invitation to the Word of God. Why do we squander our time and energy on things to fill us that leave us empty and rotten in the end? Why don't we simply listen to the Word and be truly fed and satisfied?

Isaiah goes on to describe how the Word of God has a purpose, just like the rain that falls from heaven waters the earth, so also the Word of God will water us and plant peace and joy in us.

> "As the rain and the snow come down from heaven, and do not return to it without watering the earth and making it bud and flourish, so that it yields seed for the sower and bread for the eater, so is my word that goes out from my mouth: it will not return to me empty, but will accomplish what I desire and achieve the purpose for which I sent it. You will go out in joy and be led forth in peace."
>
> ISAIAH 55:10-12

We NEED to be planting the Word first and foremost. That is the seed that offers the fruit. Without it, it is impossible to bear fruit. When we consume hours of social media and only mere minutes of the Bible then wonder why the fruit of our life is discontentment, we need to remember that what we plant we will reap.

The Word is living and active, can cut between bone and marrow (Hebrews 4:12) and is one of the ways God speaks to us. I heard a speaker recently comment that a man said "But I can't remember what I've read in the Bible." His response was, "Well I can't remember what I had for breakfast last week but it still nourished me."

Sometimes that's just how it is. We need to plant the Word even if we don't see immediate fruit. We live in such a fast-paced, instant culture that we expect everything in our lives to grow just as quickly.

We need to trust that even if we don't see the fruit right away, the seed has been planted.

There was a season in my life (University days) where I was really into this show, *Felicity.*[22] My roommate had the DVD collection (Keep in mind this was way before Netflix!) I binged watched this show before "binge watching" was even a thing!

Normally in life, when you're talking with a friend and they share about a scenario they're going through, your brain searches the rolodex of your own lifetime and tries to remember a similar situation so you can relate. At the time, I was so immersed in this show that whenever I was having a real-life conversation with a friend, my brain immediately thought of scenarios from this show, instead of *my* life. I knew it was a problem when I began a sentence for the third time in one conversation, "Oh that's just like in Felicity's life where…" Sometimes our brains are so immersed in a particular situation that we simply view all of life through that lens.

This was not actually helpful to me in any way in my relationships in university, but it can be really helpful for us when it comes to being immersed in the Word. As we read, listen to, and speak the Word it becomes part of our everyday thoughts. And when someone tells us what they are going through in their life we will have a Bible rolodex to look through that will help point us to the truth and bring encouragement.

Even if we don't see immediate fruit, even if we don't recall exactly what we read, when the Word is planted, we will be able to reap it when we need it. Jesus promised us that the Holy Spirit will remind us of God's truth.

"But the Advocate, the Holy Spirit, whom the Father will send in my name, will teach you all things and will remind you of everything I have said to you."
JOHN 14:26

Plant Silence

Never before has there been such a need to prioritize times of silence and solitude in our lives. No other generation before us had to deal with 24/7 distractions the way we do. If we aren't careful, we can be entirely consumed every waking moment.

I imagine my grandparent's lives on their farm. They did not wake up with an iPhone beside their bed as their alarm. They had time with their own thoughts as they woke and went about their morning routine.

If we're not careful, from the moment we wake, our brain can be consumed by what is going on in the world, the lives of our friends, and any number of personal and global crises. Before we have had time to brush our teeth, we sometimes hand over the peace we (hopefully) achieved during sleep and exchange it for whatever is "trending."

If we want to cultivate peace and joy in our lives, we need to create space for them to grow. The gift of silence is that it allows our brains to unwind, to decompress.

A tiny seed has a lot of needs if it is going to develop into a beautiful flower. There are things we can do to help that seed flourish. The same is true for the good things we plant in the soil of our hearts. There are things we can do to tend and cultivate those good seeds to help them grow. Silence is one of those things. And not just being quiet for the sake of quiet, but quiet with intention.

Quiet for the sake of listening to God. Quiet for the sake of being aware and inviting His healing presence into our lives.

It would be odd if I woke in the morning and did not acknowledge my spouse. If I just got up, got ready, and went about my day without taking the time to speak to and listen to this person I claim to be the most important in my life. Yet isn't that how we often are with God? We are up, we are thinking about the plans for our day, (often with our face in our phones). We are consumed with what is happening around us - kids demanding breakfast, diaper changes, or any number of random requests. The pressures of the day can mount even before our feet hit the ground. What are we stressed about? What do we need to accomplish in this day?

What would it look like to shape our mornings differently? What would it look like to acknowledge Him first and foremost? What would it look like to spend time with Him asking what He thinks about our day?

> *Jesus said "Our Father in heaven, hallowed be your name, your kingdom come, your will be done, on earth as it is in heaven. Give us today our daily bread."*
> **MATTHEW 6:9-11**

What would it look like if we started our day in this way? Your kingdom come. (Not my plans for the day.) Your will be done. (Surrendering my expectations for how this day will play out.) Give us our daily bread. (Depending on Him for everything in our day.)

Many times in the Bible we see the call to offer our first fruits. We have come to see this as simply a tithe offering, ten percent of the finances we make. What if God is calling us to so much more than a portion of our money? The first fruit of our day spent with Him. In the quiet. In the stillness.

What would He say to us in that time?

Does it have to be morning? No, but stick with me. What we plant first in our hearts in the morning will continue to grow throughout the day. If we plant stress and anxiety about all that we need to do, that will only grow stronger. If we plant fear about all that we need to face we will see the fruit of that fear-seed later. If we plant comparison and jealousy, we will not begin the day rising up as the women God has called us to be. We must plant what we want to grow. That is why I believe there is something special connected to connecting with Him first.

This is an area that does NOT come naturally to me. I have declared myself a night owl for my entire life, claiming that it was in my DNA and just "who I am." I couldn't possibly wake up a second earlier than absolutely necessary to be able to get ready for my day.

But it's amazing what can happen when we completely surrender who we think we are into the hands of a transformative God.

He created us and He can re-create us to be more than we ever thought or imagined. He has great plans for us - are we sleeping through them?

The process of beginning to wake up with Him hasn't been an easy one and it is something I can still struggle with. Sleep is so good! In various seasons, sleep is what we need to prioritize. What I have found is that when I fill myself first with Him, I have a natural outpouring for those around me. In the past I would struggle so much to drum up compassion for my children and those around me. I would have to find sources of patience and understanding that I did not naturally carry. On days where I first planted His presence and the Word, I would find this outflow from Him. What began to grow was love, joy, peace, patience, and all of the other fruits of the Spirit.

Hey there mama of little ones - this is a tough one for you. Give yourself lots of grace here. Find a time that works for you in your day. Pick an anchor in the day - nap time, or put on a show for the kids every day at 10 am and spend a bit of time with Him. I know the laundry is pressing, and the dishes are piling up, but choosing to allow God to fill our souls will give us an energy for #allthethings we need to do that cannot come from anywhere else. Also, there is no requirement of how much to read, how long to pray or what to do in this time. Simply sit with Him and allow His presence to fill you and guide you. He is not expecting performance. Maybe you can play a little worship music and close your eyes. Maybe you can read a Psalm and allow yourself to dwell on it all day. Maybe you press play on your Bible app and let the spoken Word of God fill you while you close your eyes and drift off to a peaceful nap. The truth is, the what exactly you do doesn't matter as much as that you are simply choosing to spend time with Him. This will bear deep fruit in your life that is much needed during this demanding season. Allow Him to fill the tired and weary spaces. You've got this mama!

Plant Gratefulness and Thankfulness

I recently had an experience where I was frustrated with someone in my life. I ended up sharing these frustrations with a friend. (Though I'm not advising the practice of venting or complaining.) Later on in the conversation my friend asked me a question about another area of my life and as I began to speak about this area it included ways in which I appreciated this same person that was causing frustration in my life. As I shared about the way I appreciated this person I noticed my posture shift - both in my body and in my heart. I was no longer as tangled in annoyance as I had been.

As I spoke the words of gratefulness out loud, I was changed by them.

This is a bit difficult. I don't think it's healthy to simply keep our frustrations inside. But sometimes we are overrun by them. Sometimes we allow the negative to take over. I can't feel joy if I'm complaining. *When I am thankful my heart posture shifts.*

For me thankfulness and gratefulness is a practice. It does not come naturally. But like so many other things I have noticed along this journey, the more I practice it, the easier and more natural it becomes. Planting gratefulness and thankfulness is a way I can cultivate what I want in my life. When I speak negatively or focus on the things I am frustrated with in my life, those things begin to grow in my head and in my heart.

Think about it for a moment. Think about a recent negative interaction you had with someone, whether a stranger or someone you know. If you then chose to relay that negative experience to someone else you are actually reliving that interaction. That is the process of cultivating negativity in your life. Often we do this subconsciously out of habit. We are used to sharing stories about our experiences. This doesn't mean we don't tell the people we love about the difficult moments in our day. However, there is a difference between sharing about a challenging circumstance and cultivating an atmosphere of negativity.

> *"When you speak healing words, you offer others fruit from the tree of life. But unhealthy, negative words do nothing but crush their hopes."*
> **PROVERBS 15:4 (TPT)**

When I intentionally speak words of life, hope, and truth I am choosing to plant what I want to see in my life and in the lives of those around me. This is not an easy process especially when we are in the habit of simply allowing ourselves to speak about whatever we want in any way that we want. But when we are aware that practicing self-control will benefit our own souls it does become easier.

The main challenge I find is when there is a "one-off" moment that is justified. A moment where I have a right to be angry, frustrated, and offended. But when we realize that our response to those actions and those moments will either be cultivating something inside of us that grows life or breeds death, we begin to take better care of our reactions.

This is an area that is key to keeping our gardens weed-free so we will come back to it a little more thoroughly in Week 6.

Plant Hope and Joy

Plan(t) fun. It is easy to get lost in the world of adult responsibilities and forget to simply have fun. What actually brings you joy? What delighted you as a child? For me, I have a memory of jumping on the trampoline in the summer in a bathing suit with the sprinkler going and a container of dish soap in my hand. I was simply being free to be me, to laugh and to enjoy the moment.

Have you had those moments in your adult life? They seem to be so readily available to us when we're kids, but often the responsibilities of life choke them out. We don't seem to have the time, energy, or desire to create those moments in our life. Sometimes we just don't even know what we would want to do. We will often just look to others around us to get inspiration. "Well that's what the Smiths did, so should we do that?" Or we just do what is right in front of us. "Should we go to a movie? Dinner? Watch Netflix?" None of these things are bad or wrong, but they don't always produce joy.

So, what does?

What is holding you back from pursuing what would bring you joy? I know for myself, the one holding me back from pursuing what brings me joy is _myself_. I become consumed with "What will others think?" "That doesn't seem very practical." "I'm too old to do that."

I likely won't experience the same amount of joy bouncing on a trampoline as I did when I was a kid, but what would plant joy in my life? I am often guilty of being too serious and "adulting" too hard. It's hard for me to let go and just have fun for the sake of having fun. Somewhere along the way I believed that joy was decadent, frivolous, and unattainable.

Sometimes it is because of the hand that life has dealt us. The things we have experienced and walked through seem to have sucked the life right out of us. I am always inspired when I hear stories of those around me who have suffered greatly in life yet still have managed to pursue joy with reckless abandon. These testimonies of joy despite the bleakest of circumstances show me that joy is not dependent on what has happened to me in my life, but Who is in control of my life. Hearing these stories produce seeds of hope and encourage me that despite what I have walked through or what will come my way, I can thrive because of Him. Deep, true, joy in our lives comes through deep connection with the Gardener regardless of what life throws our way.

Plant Presence

A few years ago, I noticed that I had a funny habit. I would sit down to watch TV but then after a few minutes into whatever I was watching I would pull out my phone. I'm not sure why. Was the show not very entertaining? Was I bored? Was there something I needed to "check?" Whatever the case may be, I wasn't very present while I was supposedly watching TV and often found myself not really enjoying the show. Is it any wonder that I couldn't enjoy myself while my eyes and mind were focused elsewhere?

The same can be true for many areas of my life, phone or no phone. I can allow my mind to wander toward the future or the past, fearing, regretting, wishing, and hoping. The entire time I am in one space in my life, my mind can be living in another. Our phones make this experience far too accessible.

It is incredibly difficult to experience true joy and peace in a moment when our heads and our hearts are somewhere else.

Quite simply one of the easiest ways I have found that I can plant the fruit want to see in my life is choosing to be present in the moment. When I look whoever I am with directly in the eyes and spend time listening to their conversation, or get lost in a book, or do whatever activity it is that I am doing in a fully present way, I am able to enjoy myself more fully.

Co-Workers

Ultimately, we are not the ones who produce this fruit in our lives. As we spend time with the Gardener He will begin to reveal fruit in our lives. Joy will begin to bubble up from a spring deep within. He brings the peace, He delivers hope. We are co-labourers.

"We are coworkers with God and you are God's cultivated garden, the house he is building."
1 CORINTHIANS 3:9 (TPT)

What are you waiting for? What do you want to plant in the soil of your heart? What do you want to produce in your life?

SONG: *"Joy"* by for KING & COUNTRY[23]

DISCUSSION QUESTIONS:

1) Picture yourself as a child - what brought you joy? What brings you joy today?

2) Which Fruit of the Spirit do you see evident in your life right now? Which one would you love to see grow in your life and why?

3) Plant the Word, Plant Silence, Plant Thankfulness and Gratefulness, Plant Joy and Hope, Plant Presence. Which of these do you struggle with the most? Which one comes easiest to you?

LIFEWORK:

1) Draw the garden you want to grow. Dream with God about His plans for you and your heart. What has He put in you all along? This is not optional! Make it fun, don't worry about it not looking great! Get messy and allow God to use this time of colouring to envision the soil of your heart. Begin to plant those seeds as your marker hits the paper.

2) 5-day challenge! Create a space to read the Bible every day for five days for five minutes. I strongly encourage you to find a time at the beginning of your day or at least in the middle and not leave it until the end of the night when you are tired and would rather let your brain rest. Not to say closing out the day in the Bible isn't also a good practice but we want a time when we are more alert. I recommend starting by waking up five minutes early. Feel free to read whatever you like, but I have a few passages for you if you're stuck as to where to begin. My one request is that you use a physical Bible. (No distracting notifications!)

Before you begin ask God if there's anything He'd like to show you in this passage. Extra points for reading it out loud.

- Isaiah 55

- Psalm 23

- Matthew 6:9-13 (or the whole passage)

- John chapters 1-5 (one chapter a day)

- Acts chapters 1-5 (one chapter a day)

3) Look up Romans 12:2 in at least three different translations and write down the one that most resonates with you.

Sustaining

I have three kids, the oldest of which just turned eight. I have been carrying a child either inside or outside my body for the last nine years. I feel like I should be stronger than I am. My youngest is nearly three and has hit a bit of a whiney phase. She will look up at me and demand, "Carry me!" Sigh. I pick her up once again and hold her until she is content to play on her own. If I am physically picking up a 30lb kid regularly, why don't I feel stronger? Why am I not strong?

I just got back from a month long stay at a summer camp where Brendan, was working. The distance between the dining hall and where we slept involved walking up two major hills. (This was actually a good thing as it offset the ample dessert selection!) To be honest, it was exhausting and sometimes a bit overwhelming after a meal to think about heading back up to our room with my three kids. I brought a wagon and often lugged the two littlest back to the room slowly but surely making our way home. Onlookers would applaud or gives looks of compassion as they could see what a feat it was to pull this heavy weight.

I began to look at this journey as an "exercise opportunity" instead of dreading it. Sure, it was difficult and I would end up sweaty and exhausted by the time I reached my destination. But at the end of our month long stay I felt strong. I knew that each day I was working out. I wouldn't have chosen to do this on my own. If there was an escalator option I would have hopped right on! This hill was my only choice, I had to walk up the hill to get home. I could do this feeling helpless and hopeless like it was going to destroy me, or I could see it for what it was - an opportunity to grow stronger. Now interestingly, regardless of my views in the moment, I was going to get stronger going up the hill each day, but my experience in the moment depended on me. I think this is what happens to us daily.

We can't always change the circumstances we are in but we can choose to see them as opportunities to strengthen us, or we can whine all the way up the hill.

VERSE OF THE WEEK

"So then, just as you received Christ Jesus as Lord, continue to live your lives in him, rooted and built up in him, strengthened in the faith as you were taught, and overflowing with thankfulness."

COLOSSIANS 2:6-7

Storms

I want to start off this week talking about storms. The ones we see coming, the ones we don't expect, and the ones we deal with on a regular basis. We learn to deal with life's little storms so we're prepared when the big storms come, not that we can ever be *fully prepared*, but we have roots in place. We have storm experience. We don't know the outcome but we have a firm foundation.

Our family recently had a very busy two months. Brendan was away for half of the first month and when he was home I seemed to be out. Then we had the month up at camp. Some days it felt like I saw him for five minutes. Neither of these circumstances are healthy for our relationship. But at the end of the two months we walked away strong and connected. How was that? We have spent years developing deep roots of connection that could withstand what those two months threw at us. The time we did have together we spent with intention when possible, asking good questions and listening. We had cultivated a strong foundation that could withstand a few crazy months.

This is the hope for us with our relationship with God. We don't want to wait for hard things to happen in our lives to try and figure out our relationship with Him in the midst of it. We want a firm foundation to thrive in the everyday little storms and the big ones.

We Need Storms

The angry clouds rolled in as I sat in anticipation next to the big picture window in the living room of my grandma's farmhouse. There was something so captivating about the thunder and lightning that boomed across the open prairie sky. We weren't afraid. It was a show. We were safe inside, huddled together, listening to nature run its course. As a kid I understood storms are just a part of life. But getting older I began to dread them. I had people to protect, I had something to lose if the storm was too intense. I began to build a world that avoided storms at all cost.

It didn't matter if we weren't living freely and fully - as long as we were safe.

I've come to see now that we need storms. As discouraging as that can be to say, let me explain. Storms have the ability to grow us in dependence on Him. They build our character and they help us see what is actually important in life. They move us from being helpless children to mature ones. They turn us into people who are able to choose joy amidst pain, able to praise and find freedom from the chains, and able to point others to Christ even when it is hard.

I don't know if you remember a 90's movie called "Biodome?" In it the characters accidentally get locked inside a manufactured bubble world. This idea may have been inspired by a world that was created by scientists in the late 80's and through their experimental world they discovered that...

"The trees inside Biosphere 2 grew rapidly, more rapidly than they did outside of the dome, but they also fell over before reaching maturation. After looking at the root systems and outer layers of bark, the scientists came to realize that a lack of wind in Biosphere 2 caused a deficiency of stress wood. Stress wood helps a tree position itself for optimal sun absorption and it also helps trees grow more solidly. Without stress wood, a tree can grow quickly, but it cannot support itself fully. It cannot withstand normal wear and tear, and survive. In other words, the trees needed some stress in order to thrive in the long run."[24]

The trees could grow, but they were not able to fully stand without the wind making them strong.

> *"Consider it pure joy, my brothers and sisters, whenever you face trials of many kinds, because you know that the testing of your faith produces perseverance."*
>
> **JAMES 1:2-3**

I have always hated this verse. I don't want to face trials. I want life to be easy. I think this is something we can all agree on! Why would James write this? Why would he tell us to consider it joy? It seems like one more backwards thing about this Kingdom of God.

"The testing of your faith develops perseverance." (vs. 3) We need the testing to make our faith stronger. The word for testing in Greek is **dokimion**[25] which can be defined as "that by which something is tried or proved, a test." Have you ever asked someone to "prove it?" When you have to prove something it takes work. It also builds evidence and makes it stronger. Can you prove your faith?

This word perseverance in Greek is **hypomonē**[26]. One description is "the characteristic of a man who is not swerved from his deliberate purpose and his loyalty to faith and piety by even the greatest trials and sufferings." This is what trials have the ability to do. They have the ability to strengthen us in a way unlike any other. But they can also break us.

Sometimes that outcome - strengthen or break - is up to us and the state of our hearts.

Strong Hearts are Soft

Have you ever been caught in a storm in a tropical country? Often those storms come hard and fast. I live outside of Vancouver in Canada and sometimes it is referred to as "Rain-couver" because of the heavy amount of precipitation we receive each year. Here's the funny thing; I rarely see people walking around with rain jackets, rain boots, and umbrellas. I guess because we are used to this rain, and often it isn't too intense. We will get a steady, slow, rain, but not usually the kind of rain that drenches you in seconds. Downpours happen in tropical places. The skies open up and pour down intensely, and often it passes quickly.

I was in Hawaii a few years ago when my phone pinged with an alert. I looked down and was relieved that it was simply an intense rainfall warning and not something more serious. How helpful would it be if we had similar technology warning us of the storms about to appear in our own lives? Ping! You are about to get a life-changing phone call. Ping! You are about to experience a health crisis. Maybe those texts wouldn't be so helpful, but often storms in life happen so quickly and without warning we are left reeling, simply trying to survive.

After the rain storm I experienced in Hawaii I was amazed at all of the debris strewn throughout the property where we were staying. Bits of garbage and huge palm branches were littered all around. As I looked up, I was in awe of the palm trees proudly standing tall as if nothing had happened at all. Sure, they lost a few branches in the process but they had not been broken themselves. They had withstood the storm.

Do you know much about palm trees? Do you know that the very cells that make up a palm tree are malleable? They are designed to bend and sway. In the Pacific North West our trees often come crashing down during violent windstorms. Even thick, old, sturdy trees will fall if the wind is mighty enough. These trees are hard. They were not created to bend and sway.[27]

That is how it is with our hearts. Hard hearts are prone to be destroyed when the storms of life come. We harden our hearts to protect them. When the storms of life come raging, we erect walls of protection, often unconsciously. Do you remember a moment when you were rejected by a friend in high school? A moment where you didn't make a sports team, or were dumped by a boyfriend? We often make silent vows to ourselves that we will never again experience pain like that so we do things to keep ourselves safe.

We choose to keep people at a distance and decide that we have to be the ones in charge of our own safety and well-being.

Our hearts can become hard through the circumstances in our life, when we hold onto unforgiveness and when we hold onto our "rights." Hearts that have built up walls of bitterness, resentment, jealousy, entitlement, anger, and discontentment are destroyed when the blows of life hit them. Walls are built so we will not experience pain or suffering. We hold onto control so tightly, hoping to keep everyone in our life safe and free from pain, and when something difficult happens and the illusion of control is ripped from our hands, we are crushed by it.

Do you know what happens when I try and remove a weed from my garden and the soil is rock hard? It is nearly impossible. That dense, firm soil has a grip on that weed that will not let go. Weeds are removed far easier when the soil is soft. And what softens the soil? Rain. Storms come and the rain beats down on the ground making the soil loose. I am able to uproot weeds in my garden far easier than when the soil is hard and firm. When we can allow the circumstances in our lives to turn us to God, our soil is loosened. When we surrender our control to Him, our heart begins to soften, and He is able to remove the weeds from our heart. I sometimes wonder if a storm comes our way so that God can remind us that He is in control. This is why soft hearts are so important. God loves soft hearts.

Often we get caught up in trying to "do" better and "be" better Christians. God's main concern is always with our heart. *"I will give you a new heart and put a new spirit in you; I will remove from you your heart of stone and give you a heart of flesh." Ezekiel 36:26*

Who Sent the Storm?

Sometimes I can spend all of my energy in a storm trying to figure out where it came from. Is God bringing something my way to grow me or point me in a new direction? Is the enemy sending a flaming arrow? Are these circumstances a consequence of my own actions?

In Mark 4:35-41 we see Jesus and the disciples on a boat when a storm suddenly appears. Jesus is asleep on the boat and everyone, understandably freaks out, and wakes Him up. He gets up, rebukes the wind and it immediately dies down. Take a minute to read this story.

The Greek word for rebuke is **epitimaō**[28] and is the same word Jesus uses when He rebukes demons and unclean spirits. It seems as though this storm suddenly appeared to keep Jesus from going to the other side of the lake. What was on the other side? A man who needed Him. A man that was tormented by unclean spirits.

Is it possible a storm comes to distract us from what we are supposed to do?

It took just one word from Jesus's mouth to shut down that storm so He could carry on with His journey. I think there are some storms in our lives that need to be shut down. Things that are causing a distraction from the plans and the purpose for our lives. He has given us the authority as sons and daughters of God to use His Name to rebuke things in our lives that are causing storms.

Another Storm

Are you familiar with the story of Jonah? If not - pause this and head over to read it (four very short chapters, a 5-10 minute read).

> *"He went aboard and sailed for Tarshish to flee from the Lord. Then the Lord sent a great wind on the sea, and such a violent storm arose that the ship threatened to break up."*
>
> **JONAH 1:3-4**

Wait, wait, wait. Hold on. God sent the storm? To be honest this isn't an easy section to write. I have heard many times that God doesn't cause any pain or heartache, but only that He will use all of the difficulties in our lives for His glory. But He sent it?

And there are other places I see Him bringing something less than ideal into people's lives. Take for example Saul in 1 Samuel 16:14 where it says God sent an evil spirit to torment him. Or Isaiah 45:7 which says *"I bring prosperity and create disaster."* Or how about Haggai 2:17 *"I struck all the work of your hands with blight, mildew and hail, yet you did not return to me,' declares the Lord."*

I want to say delicately that I simply don't have all of the answers and that is okay. I want to offer what I believe is happening here. I believe God will make our lives a bit uncomfortable as a means of drawing us back to Him.

I think if we are quiet and take the time with Him, we can begin to discern if God trying to get our attention in some way. If that is the case, it is always out of love. It is always out of a desire to bring us back in line with Him because He has good plans for our lives.

Is God trying to get our attention? Is He wanting to re-align us with His will and His plans for our lives? This isn't a very popular view. While I think most of the storms we face in life are simply because we live in a broken and fallen world, there are a number of times we see that God is sending something in the way of a storm in someone's life to get their attention. Not to needlessly harm them, that is not in His character, but to draw them back to Him.

If you did just read the story of Jonah maybe you were surprised as I was to read the last chapter. I don't remember that part of the story from the flannelgraph in Sunday School. We don't often focus on this part of the story. We know God wanted to re-route Jonah, we know he had a purpose to play, but how he continues to respond to God is interesting. Things didn't "work out" for Jonah the way he wanted. Behind the scenes we continue to see God's hand in his life.

- God *provided* the shade (4:6) Jonah was happy about it.

- God *provided* the worm (4:7) Jonah was unhappy.

- God *provided* a scorching east wind (4:8) Jonah wanted to die.

Provision: The same word is used for the fish (1:17) the thing that saved Jonah's life. Sometimes God's provision doesn't look appealing. Sometimes he is saving us from a storm but we can't see it. *Sometimes He is trying to change us on the inside.*

Do we sometimes not change? Do we sometimes continue to resist even after He realigns us? It is *really* difficult for us to give up control. If I'm really honest, I have a hard time giving up control. And I think that's how I sometimes end up in another kind of storm.

The Storms We Create

The tricky thing about the storms in life is that it is hard to discern where they came from. Is the enemy coming against me? Is God trying to get my attention? Or maybe, I am just walking through the consequence of my own actions.

The third storm I want to highlight is found in Acts 27:9-44. Paul, a prisoner, is sailing to Rome and warns those in charge that if they carry on the way they are going they will encounter a storm and experience loss. They choose not to heed Paul's advice and keep going. Take a minute and read about this storm.

What we see in this storm is that it could have been avoided! Have you ever had an experience in your life where you knew you were walking into something that wasn't wise? Just like the sailors in this story, I often believe I simply know what is best for my life and I decide to plow on ahead instead of listening to the voice of wisdom.

> *And then, just like the crew in this boat, I find myself caught up in a storm and I realize it could have been avoided, but now I am faced with the consequences.*

Sometimes the "financial storm" I experience in my life is due to poor choices I have made with my money. I knew I didn't have the money to go on that trip, buy those clothes, or go to that restaurant but I decided to sail right into that storm anyways.

Living with the consequences of our own actions is not fun. But I have found that when I can accept them and learn from them, rather than try and run from them, the storm is able to pass much more quickly.

I have also found that when I come to Him with the storm I find myself in, then He is able to help me turn things around. He is able to give me wisdom, resources, and strength to do what is necessary to turn my ship around.

The turning point for Paul's crew was in verse 35 where they pause and Paul gives thanks. This is the moment where they chose not to rely on their own wisdom and desire to control but to acknowledge the One who is in control. From that point on they had the courage to do what was necessary for their survival. It meant a loss of their ship, but God was partnering with them to save their lives.

> *And once we partner with Him and allow Him to direct and re-direct us, He is able to sustain us in a way we could not on our own.*

I love in the next chapter of Acts where the crew has run ashore on an island and it says *"The islanders showed us unusual kindness."* (Acts 28:2) Isn't that just like God? Once we surrender our plans He is able to provide for us in ways that even seem unusually kind.

I don't know if you find yourself walking through one of those storms right now. They're not fun. They can feel embarrassing and shameful. We should have known better. But remember what we discussed in Week One; shame does not come from God. It is not His plan for our lives to walk around in guilt and shame. When something comes to light, we have the opportunity to partner with God to make it right. He longs to bring things to the light to help us walk freely and lightly.

Fearing the Storms of Life

I have a stockpile of flashlights from a big storm that never came, well it came, but not really the way I expected. There was this huge storm that was supposed to hit two years ago. There was a lot of buildup in the news. "Get your house ready, stock up on water and flashlights. Be prepared for power outages."

This wouldn't normally freak me out too much, but the storm was supposed to hit while Brendan was away for the weekend so I would be alone with the kids, and Noelle was only a few months old. I was incredibly sleep deprived and experiencing Postpartum depression. I remember the night before he left, I went to the store in a panic. I bought $70 worth of flashlights and other storm gear. I wanted to be prepared.

Friday came and just as Brendan was preparing to leave the house the power went out. I was already bawling due to a combination of hormones, and feeling abandoned in my time of need, but this sent me into full-on psycho-mama panic mode.

A friend of mine had offered to have us at her house for the weekend because their power hardly ever went out, and even if it did, I wouldn't be alone. I frantically packed like a person whose house was about to be hit by a fast approaching fire. I wasn't thinking clearly and threw anything and everything we could possibly need into our suitcases. We arrived at my friend's house and I still remember the shocked look on her husband's face as he greeted me at the van and offered to help carry my things inside. He must have thought I was moving in!

It was a crazy weekend. To give the other family a bit of breathing room I decided to take my crew home on Saturday afternoon to nap and hang out. As it turned out our power had only been off for about an hour on the Friday. It was a bit windy outside, but it didn't really feel like anything too dramatic. I felt a little silly for my Friday afternoon panic-mode.

While everyone was having a rest suddenly my oldest daughter began to feel sick. She's always been a bit of a "puker" so I wasn't too worried but it was obvious we wouldn't be able to go back to my friend's place to sleep that night. We were safely tucked in at home, but without our stuff. I felt stuck at home with a sleeping newborn, a stubborn toddler and a sick kid. I had to somehow figure out how to "schlep" all of them into the van, drive 20 minutes to pack up the monster amount of stuff at my friend's, and then trek it all back home again. This felt like the real storm.

Storms on the outside are always dealt with on the inside.

I had let the circumstances around me turn me into an overly stressed out person who did not know how to make wise decisions. This wasn't the first time this had happened. This was a pattern in my life. When things got overwhelming, I had a few classic responses.

1) I would shut down, totally paralyzed by the stress I was facing. I would hide away and try to find any means of escape. Procrastinating things I needed to do, stress building inside of me as I avoided

what I needed to do by doing other "good" things, like cleaning my room, making a healthy meal or exercising. Sometimes my choices were not as positive as I would escape into a world of TV or food and drink to comfort what felt depressing to me, or heavy in my heart. I've come to realize sometimes that heaviness is simply stress in disguise.

2) Another response was a rush of tears. I would become overly emotional, often blaming others for what was happening *to* me. Somehow if I could shift responsibility off myself then I wouldn't have to feel the responsibility or the guilt of what was going on around me.

3) Lastly, I would often respond with anger. This was also connected to blame. I wanted to be angry at whoever I felt was responsible for the situation I found myself in. In this case it was my husband's fault for abandoning me in my time of need. While the circumstances weren't ideal, my emotions or overwhelm weren't his fault.

> *While the storms in life can be exasperated by others around me, (sometimes storms are the fault of others) I cannot hold them responsible for my response or my actions.*

In the case of the "big storm" weekend, another friend came to my rescue, watching the kids at my house while I was able to retrieve our stuff. In the end everything turned out okay. We didn't lose power again and Laurel recovered from her sickness. I did, however, let the thought of the oncoming storm get the best of me.

That happens sometimes. In the middle of a storm we turn into the worst version of ourselves.

Are you familiar with the song *"New Wine"* by Hillsong Worship?[29] Here are some of the lyrics:

> *In the crushing*

> *In the pressing*

> *You are making new wine*

> *In the soil I now surrender*

> *You are breaking new ground*

This is what the storms of life feel like. They feel like an inside crushing. Sometimes we physically feel like we can't breathe. Just like the "big storm" turned me into the worst version of myself, this is what often happens to us when we feel this way. When we feel crushed and pressed.

The truth is, I don't often get to the place of surrender. I don't often give God a chance to turn a storm into "new wine." I settle for the vinegar that I'm used to producing.

If we can't choose joy and lean on Him during the small storms of life, how can we expect to when the bigger storms hit? If we don't have faith that He will come through for us in the small things life throws our way, how will we be able to depend on Him during the big things? Life's daily, little storms need to be treated with the same respect. We need to continue to choose joy despite having a "right" to be angry, despite hurt and pain, despite being wronged.

> *We need to use the "wind" of the daily trials of life to strengthen our roots.*
> *We need to be intentional about growing deep root systems to*
> *ground us when the bigger storms come our way.*

Let's unpack this for a minute. I am not the most veteran mother out there. I have three girls, the oldest of which is eight. I have over 2,920 parenting days under my belt. What I have discovered in the raising of each of my children is that they share a few things in common. They start off completely helpless and I have to do everything for them. Slowly and steadily they become more independent. They begin to feed themselves, dress themselves and eventually go to the bathroom all on their own. (Let all God's people say Amen!)

There is always this awkward phase that kicks in around the age of two where they long to be independent yet don't have the skills to do anything. It is a point where they struggle with car seat buckles and Velcro straps and I do my best to assist where I can. They need to overcome this struggle to be able to master this difficult task that is seemingly too big and too overwhelming for them.

Often I hear this loud whining or moaning coming from a child who is independently struggling with something and I come to them and say, "Can I help you? Would you like help? Why didn't you ask for help?" I always wonder, why have you struggled to the point of utter despair and frustration when I have been here all along able to help you? I think God looks at us the same way. We find ourselves in a struggle, a storm or a battle, trying to go it alone.

Is it possible God is waiting for us to turn to Him? To look to Him?
To ask for His help, His guidance, His hand?

We can spend our entire lives living in fear of "the big storm." Something we are terrified of can leave us paralyzed at just the thought of it occurring. When we do this, we can experience the storms of life over and over again emotionally and even physically without them ever occurring! We can let fear overtake us and shut us down similarly to how I responded to "the big storm."

Often, I believe, we anticipate these storms or "biggest fears" in our lives believing they will destroy us. When we anticipate walking through them without God we end up spending energy battling events that aren't real.

In some ways, all of life is a storm. Life is difficult. If we left it there, I would be incredibly depressed and want to give up. But we don't leave it there because life isn't the end. When we feel awkward and uncomfortable in our own skin, I think that is okay. This isn't really our home. We should feel at least a little "off" here. I believe God wants to give us true contentment and an abundant life as we surrender fully to Him. He has a "storm free" home waiting for us. Ultimately, that is what helps us withstand any storm. Our faith and our trust is not in this place, it is not in any person or any circumstance. Ultimately our faith is in Him and His plans for us.

> *"For I know the plans I have for you," declares the Lord, "plans to prosper you and not to*
> *harm you, plans to give you hope and a future."*
> **JEREMIAH 29:11**

He has good plans for us, but do we get in our own way? Do we really believe this promise?

I want to try a little exercise. When you read this verse, I want you to insert your name.

> *"For I know the plans I have for you," _____" plans to prosper you and not to harm*
> *you, plans to give you hope and a future."*
> **JEREMIAH 29:11**

Do you believe this? Take a few minutes to search your heart. Do you believe that God has good plans for you and for your life? Or have life's storms crushed your spirit?

> *"The Lord is close to the brokenhearted, and saves those who are crushed in spirit."*
> **PSALM 34:18**

Even when we're crushed He is there. It does not mean storms won't come, it means we won't be alone. I was walking through one of my hardest storms two years ago. I hadn't been really reading my Bible. I wasn't not reading it, I just wasn't reading it. Somehow during that time I flipped to another verse in Jeremiah, *"I have loved you with an everlasting love; I have drawn you with unfailing kindness. I will build you up again, and you Virgin Israel, will be rebuilt. Again you will take up your timbrels and go out to dance with the joyful." (31:3-4)* Though I was in an incredibly dark season I took that promise as my own. I held onto it. I would experience joy again.

During that season in my life the weather outside seemed to match how I was feeling on the inside. The sky was gray and rain poured down as often as my tears. Though the season felt like it would never end I had a small sliver of hope. I knew I would *"Dance with the joyful" (Jeremiah 31:4)* again. As I drove alone one afternoon for a brief moment the sun popped out and shone directly on my face. This felt like a special gift just for me. It was a small step towards that promise of joy. Even in my dark valley, He was there.

When our roots are deep and our hearts are soft, we can withstand the storms of life. We may feel pain, (I imagine a palm tree getting absolutely destroyed throughout the night). Yet in the morning there it is, standing tall in the sunlight. A few branches missing and it is a little beaten up, but it is still standing.

SONG: *"Praise Before My Breakthrough"* by Bryan & Katie Torwalt[30]

DISCUSSION QUESTIONS:

1) Have you ever been caught in a storm you didn't expect? What was your experience?

2) Is there a storm that has happened in your life that is still leaving you feeling a little crushed? If you're working through this study as a group, pause to pray about this storm. (If not, add to your Lifework to pray with a trusted friend about this storm.) Pray that you will be able to give over the broken pieces of your heart and that you will be able to see Him in the midst of this storm.

3) Are you currently walking in a storm season? How do you think God is trying to strengthen you during this time?

LIFEWORK:

1) Is there still a storm from your past you are having trouble letting go of? Is there an outstanding offence from someone? A disappointment? A loss?

Spend some time with God this week giving over your hurt, your anger, and your pain. Don't be afraid to wrestle with Him for a bit and tell Him all of the words your heart is feeling. It will be better to get it out with Him than with anyone else. Ask Him to help begin repairing the damage that was done. Ask Him to speak life and blessing into those places that have been damaged. I know this isn't easy. This is painful, difficult work. His work in your life will not return void. Beautiful flowers will begin to grow where there were once only painful weeds.

Read Psalm 23 out loud and notice all of the actions God takes to be with us through our dark valleys. Write down this Psalm and underline each of these actions.

2) Create declarations or affirmations to speak out loud over yourself this week. You can personalize them but I am going to provide you with a few suggestions. Figure out how you are going to remember to say these. It could be Post-it notes in the bathroom mirror, or an alert on your phone. Say each declaration five times out loud. Yes, you might feel a little silly doing this, but the more we speak life and truth over ourselves the more our brain begins to believe it. These are God's promises of who we are. The enemy is trying hard to have us believes lies about ourselves and this is where we need to get on the offensive and begin to build ourselves up from the inside out

Examples:

I am a child of God. (John 1:12)

I am chosen. (Ephesians 1:4)

I am a new creation. (2 Corinthians 5:17)

I am His masterpiece. (Ephesians 2:10)

1 -

2 -

3 -

4 -

5 -

3) One of the ways we can strengthen our roots is to remember. Look back and see where God has been working in your life; protecting you, comforting you, and walking with you even when you didn't know Him.

Ask the Holy Spirit to join you as you look back on your life. Jot down any memories you have where God has been with you. Write down storms you have walked through, miracles, anything that God has done. Feel free to make this messy and random, and then try to create a good copy where you can keep this as a reminder. You will then have a tangible way to remember all that He has carried you through and all that He will carry you through.

4) Take some time to pray. Are there any areas of the "root" systems that you need to pursue?

Healthy Community

Church

Prayer

Sabbath

Bible Study

Take some action towards growing one of those roots and write it down here. Do you need to make a plan to go to church this Sunday? Do you need to have a nap or plan for a Sabbath day? It doesn't matter what you decide to do but only that you follow through with it. Remember things don't happen unless we plan them. We won't change our fruit unless we change our seed. We need to do things a little differently and more intentionally if we want to see an actual change.

Fight or flight. This is our bodies natural response. When faced with fear, frustration, agitation, or confrontation, we want to either lash out or run away. This world gives us every opportunity to feel that way.

Our culture seems to be set in "us vs them." And the "them" can change moment to moment. Is it the person on the road who doesn't seem to know how to signal? Is it the person on the other end of the phone who doesn't share our first language? Is it the person in the comments section who disagrees with our opinion? Or is it someone who simply offends us by their choices and lifestyle?

Whether we choose fight or flight our weapons are the same. Bows thrown over our shoulder and arrows pointing at the target through our words. If we have grown up in the church, we are clever as we take our shot. We would never stand out in the open declaring our attack. We hide behind our camouflage of phrases. "I'm concerned about her." "How is so and so doing?" Or we may simply discuss how wrong others are in their views, opinions, attitudes and behaviours.

And what about behind the safety of a screen? How many of us have unleashed the power of our words without facing anyone at all?

VERSE OF THE WEEK

"But if you continue to criticize and come against each other over minor issues, you're acting like wild beasts trying to destroy one another! As you yield freely and fully to the dynamic life and power of the Holy Spirit, you will abandon the cravings of your self-life. For your self-life craves the things that offend the Holy Spirit and hinder him from living free within you!"

GALATIANS 5:15-17 (TPT)

Words

I take words very seriously at our house. Especially when they are spoken between sisters. Not that long ago I overheard a disagreement between our two oldest girls. One had spoken unkindly and apologies were needed. She went through the routine of saying she was sorry, the other sister offered forgiveness and it was all wrapped up with an Instagram worthy hug.

Here's the thing. I wasn't okay. Her offence, her words at her sister had hurt me as well. I needed an apology to make things right.

I realized that must be how God feels. We, as His kids, will tear down our brothers and sisters. We are not just hurting our relationship with others in this way; we are hurting our relationship with Him. I was reminded of this recently through the story of the prodigal son. When he returns to his father he states, *"Father I have sinned against heaven and against you." (Luke 15:21)* The offence we cause on earth has a Heavenly reach.

How routinely do we hurt each other? How often do we feel a slight or an offence?

Although I knew gossiping and slandering was wrong because it hurt the person being spoken about, I began to realize that it actually hurt me more.

> *When I spoke negatively about someone else I was planting a seed of bitterness, anger, jealousy or discontentment inside the soil of my own heart.*

Are you familiar with the Ephesians 4:27? It talks about not giving the devil a foothold. I definitely didn't want to do that. But I didn't get it. How was I doing that? When I read the same verse in the Amplified translation it says, *"And do not give the devil an opportunity [to lead you into sin by holding a grudge, or nurturing anger, or harbouring resentment, or cultivating bitterness]"* I had an "aha moment." I began to notice a connection in my life between anxious and depressive feelings shortly after I had spent any time talking about someone or complaining. It was as if when I did that, I opened a door in my heart and invited the enemy in to take a seat. I had no idea holding a grudge or cultivating bitterness were allowing this to happen.

Proverbs 18:21 says, *"The tongue has the power of life and death, and those who love it will eat its fruit."* The words I spoke didn't just have the power of life and death over others, they held the power of life and death over me! I was slowly killing myself from the inside out with my words.

This doesn't just apply to gossip and slander, complaining was a huge issue for me. When I would complain, the spiral towards self-pity and depression was incredibly close at hand. It was almost like an a = b equation in my life. Complaining cultivated a negative spirit within me and resulted in self-pity, and self-pity nearly always ended in depression. Once I let myself lie down in the pit of depression it was incredibly difficult to find my way out again.

> *By taking better control of the words I spoke, I was simultaneously improving my attitude and the thoughts in my mind.*

But I can't control the words coming out of my mouth if my heart is still full of junk. *"For the mouth speaks what the heart is full of." Matthew 12:34* This is why we are focusing so much on what is going on in our heart. It has a direct correlation to what comes out of our mouth. And that has a direct correlation to what is going on in our heads.

This is a big part of keeping the garden of our heart weed-free. We know the enemy is going to try and be subtle and sneaky about how he comes along and attempts to plant weeds. Our job is to be wise about keeping the door to our heart closed off to him. We need to guard our heart.

The best defense for our heart is the Breastplate of Righteousness. (Ephesians 6:14) Think about it; a breastplate is basically a shield we have in place to protect our most valuable asset - our heart. This breastplate is held in place by righteousness. When we choose to act outside of righteousness, we open ourselves up to an attack by the enemy in this space. Imagine that every time you choose to act in an unrighteous way your breastplate slips down a little and exposes a piece of your heart. This makes you vulnerable to all sorts of flaming arrows from the enemy.

It's not about legalism. I think that's where so many of us have gotten stuck. We somehow have equated the Christian life with being really good moral people to earn some invisible gold stars. Eventually we either get exhausted or rebel. But maybe, like me, you've had an incorrect view of righteousness. It's not about doing better or being better to earn something. We can't. We can never ever, ever, ever do anything to earn God's love. That is part of the beauty of Christ taking on all of our sin and shame. We cannot do anything but receive.

For some of us we can get stuck here. "I can't do anything; so I will do nothing." We allow ourselves to do and say whatever we want under that banner of "salvation." While salvation is not in question, our ability to thrive here on earth is.

You cannot earn God's love, but it doesn't mean He doesn't care about your actions. It isn't because He's just trying to polish you up to be the best version of yourself, but because it really does make a huge difference in your heart.

> "What truly contaminates a person is not what he puts into his mouth but what comes out of his mouth. That's what makes people defiled." Then his disciples approached him and said, "Don't you know that what you just said offended the Pharisees?" Jesus replied, "Every plant that my heavenly Father didn't plant is destined to be uprooted."
>
> **MATTHEW 15:11-13 (TPT)**

What goes on in our heart affects our mind. For a lot of us we are just so sick of feeling like we are tangled in our mind. Anxious, fearful and depressive thoughts can feel like "This is just how my mind works." What if you can be free from some of this as you begin to partner with Jesus to remove the weeds hanging out in your heart?

What if vs What is

When I was pregnant with my second daughter, I remember telling the midwife I often felt like a certain pang in my side meant my baby had died in my womb. I asked her, "But everyone thinks like that right?" She assured me they did not and booked me an appointment with a therapist. As I spoke to this counsellor, she shed a bit of light on my thinking. I was a "jump to the worst conclusion" sort of person. If there was going to be an outcome in a situation, I automatically assumed the worst would happen. She not only revealed my negative thought patterns but helped me reframe my thoughts. Instead of viewing each and every pang in my pregnancy as sure death, she encouraged me to say the following, "I am so thankful for this healthy life growing inside of me." I began to train my mind to focus on what was true and good instead of what was negative and "what if."

Paul encourages us to do the same as well, *"So keep your thoughts continually fixed on all that is authentic and real, honourable and admirable, beautiful and respectful, pure and holy, merciful and kind. And fasten your thoughts on every glorious work of God, praising him always," Philippians 4:8 (TPT)*

I had read this verse before but hadn't taken notice of the call to pay attention to what was true. How often was I simply paying attention to things that "could" be, rather than what was? When I allow my mind to focus on "what if's," I plant the seeds of worry and anxiety. When I focus on what is true and what is good, I plant seeds of hope and gratefulness. Cultivating the soil of our hearts begins with our minds.

> *"Do not conform to the pattern of this world but be transformed by the renewing of your mind. Then you will be able to test and approve what God's will is - his good, pleasing and perfect will."*
> **ROMANS 12:2**

Transformed is the Greek word **metamorphoō**[31], which means "to change into another form."

Renewing is the Greek word **anakainōsis**[32], which means "a renewal, renovation, complete change for the better."

Your mind will be completely renovated and as a result you will be a completely new person. Not only that but you will have a more complete sense of God's purpose for your life. Are you confused about what you should be doing with your life? Allow your mind to be renewed and transformed and He will make it clear.

But how? How do we renew our mind? First, by reading the Bible. The Word cleanses us (Ephesians 5:26), and it is alive and active, sharp enough to divide between our soul and spirit, and judges our thoughts and attitudes of our heart (Hebrews 4:12). Nothing is more powerful in renewing our mind than reading the Word of God for ourselves. If you want to see a true change and breakthrough in your life, this is the best place to start.

As we read the Word daily and meditate on what we have read, we will notice that certain verses seem to be highlighted to us. We may feel a heaviness or a burning in our hearts as we read. This is one way in which God speaks to us.

When we are in a habit of trusting and believing who He says He is through His Word we will begin to be transformed from the inside out and having the Word deeply planted in our hearts helps us as we walk through the storms of life.

But what if we don't really trust God and His Word?

Our View of God

This is possibly one of the single most important things we can discuss. What is our view of God? For a long time, too long really, I believed God was waiting to drop a bomb on me. I believed that if I didn't hold onto everything myself, if I really gave it over to Him then He would use whatever I gave Him to punish me or test me. I'm not sure where this theology came from but I'm guessing it was a medley from my upbringing. Not one person or church's fault, but the puzzle pieces I was given.

Unfortunately, the pieces I put together left me with a view of God as just wanting to test me. As I got a bit older, I began to see that life was not all roses as I had imagined. Real, hard things were happening to people around me. I realized I had another false narrative of God. He was simply here to make my life easy and happy. When bad things happened in people's lives around me, that view of God was crushed. Was God real? Could I believe in a God that would allow ____ to happen? The truth is, I didn't really know God. I tried to piecemeal Him together with what I heard other people say about Him.

The problem is that other people are not God.
They are other broken people also trying to figure out God.

The God of my childhood seemed so angry. He was wiping people out with a flood, destroying nations through war, collapsing entire cities with a loud cry, and turning people into pillars of salt.

I think a lot of people who grew up similarly to me have held on to this powerful, scary version of God and lived not from a place of holy fear but rather, actual fear.

Others I have known simply jumped on over to the New Testament and began to pick and choose the kindest, most loving views of Jesus as God incarnate and took that image on of God as simply loving, with no wrath.

The problem with these pictures of God is that they are incomplete and not entirely correct. Only as I began to re-read the Bible for myself, the Old Testament and the New, I saw God pursuing the Israelites out of love. Yes, they continued to forget about God again and again, and yes, He was angry with them again and again but He always found a way to bring them back. Ultimately He found a way to restore all of humanity to Himself, *through* Himself.

We cannot begin to know about God until we know God.

Personally.

Until we begin to make our relationship with God our own, we will continue to be confused about who He is.

"But what about you?" he asked. "Who do you say I am?"
MATTHEW 16:15

As we begin to spend time with God, not only do we discover more about who He is but He begins to reveal to us more about who we are. In this passage of Scripture Jesus is talking to His friends that He has been walking alongside for three years. He asks them who they think He is. As one of His closest friends, Peter, declares that Jesus is indeed the Messiah, Jesus responds to Him by declaring back exactly who Peter is. Though Peter is someone who makes mistakes, denies Jesus, is outspoken and seems to fumble many times, Jesus is not looking for perfection. He is looking for someone who sees who He is. Someone who knows His heart. He in turn wants to declare over us who we are.

Have you heard the phrase "Call out the gold in others?" It's this idea that when you are with others you would call out of them the incredible things you see inside of them, even those things that are not quite who they are yet. I believe this is what God wants to do with us. He wants to speak life and truth over us and to us and to declare who we really are to ourselves. He did this with Peter and He wants to do that with you and I.

But are we listening?

Where Two are Tangled

I shared at the very beginning of this study the idea of being tangled. Much like a pair of headphones, it is often unclear how we got there and difficult to try and get untangled again. Recently I had two pairs of headphones tangled together. If you thought one pair was a pain to untangle, two is far more complicated.

Unfortunately for many of us, though we are trying to walk a fairly tangle-free life, the tangling of others gets us all caught up again.

Do you know why my kids speak English at home and not Chinese or French? Because I speak English. They pick up what I say. Lately, Noelle at 2.5 years old has been saying "oy yoy yoy" which is a favourite saying of mine. I didn't sit her down one day to say, "Okay Noelle when something disastrous or overwhelming happens copy me, say my little catch phrase." Nope. She just picked it up from spending time with me. We develop the same language as the people we spend time with. If everyone around us is speaking negatively, slandering, gossiping or simply speaking untruth then we will also begin to do so. It will become planted in our hearts and make its way up to our head and out our mouth.

> "Therefore, since we are surrounded by such a great cloud of witnesses, let us throw off everything that hinders and the sin that so easily entangles. And let us run with perseverance the race marked out for us."
>
> **HEBREWS 12:1**

Everything that hinders is the Greek word **ogkos**[33]. It refers to "whatever is prominent, a burden, a weight." What is heavy in your life? What is getting you down? What is tangling you?

Sometimes those things that bring us comfort are actually keeping us stuck, keeping us tangled.

What do you need to throw off? Is it a habit? A relationship?

Lighten the Load

I am always so amazed at physics. I don't understand physics but I am amazed by things like gravity, buoyancy etc. On land I could never possibly pick up my husband; if we were in a pool, I could more easily lift him up.

Sometimes the things that are dragging us down can't completely disappear. Sometimes they are family members, circumstances, finances, and relationships. We get so bogged down by them. They are heavy, and they are weight bearing. We were never meant to carry those things on our own. Still, we try to and we buckle under the weight. We aren't supposed to carry the stuff of life on our shoulders - He is.

When we surrender the things that weigh us down to Him, He surrounds us as if we were in a pool of water. The things we need to carry aren't gone, they become manageable. Similar to carrying my husband, it's not necessarily lightweight, there can still be a heaviness in what we carry, but when He gives us the buoyancy, it is He who does the heavy lifting.

One year for Christmas I was given a pair of soft, Velcro, ankle weights. It was the early 90's - don't judge.

I think I must have been inspired by a Jane Fonda workout tape. I would lie on my side, bright blue weights firmly strapped around my boney little ankles and I would do these leg lifts. 1, 2, 3, 4, 5...around the 10-count mark I would feel the burn and flip over. Now I don't actually know what I was thinking. I wasn't trying to lose any weight as I was an incredibly skinny little kid, but I was athletic and I think I was trying to build stronger muscle. Here's the thing I do remember. Once I took those bad boys off and tried to do the same exercise my leg would fly into the air with so much power! Once I threw off that weight I could fly. The same is true for us. When we finally are able to throw off what has been hindering us, we will be so light and free, it will feel like we are flying in life.

So many of us have been walking around wearing invisible backpacks. We travel along in our lives and begin to put things inside. Hurt and pain - throw it in, un-met expectations, disappointments and doubt - yep, unforgiveness and offence - get in there, shame, bitterness, and anger - hop in guys everyone is waiting. And we walk around so, so heavy. We have no idea we have been carrying these backpacks until we put them down and begin to unpack. "What?! I had no idea this was in there!" We release the things we were never intended to carry and life begins to get lighter.

Looking again at that verse in Hebrews 12 in The Message it says:

> "Strip down, start running—and never quit! No extra spiritual fat, no parasitic sins.
> Keep your eyes on Jesus, who both began and finished this race we're in."

I don't know about you but I was not expecting to read the words "strip down" in the Bible! But it's right here. Take it off! Let go! Get rid of all of that junk!

The second part of this verse refers to the sin that so easily entangles. We started off this course talking a lot about gardening and weeds and I want to bring us back there. If your gardening experience is limited, you'll have to do a lot of imagining with me.

The first year my mom and I really started to tackle my (mini) garden we planted a hydrangea. I didn't know much about this plant, only that I liked the look of it. In its first year I loved how it bloomed and couldn't wait to see what it looked like the following year. I had heard if you changed the soil contents the blooms changed colour. I was curious to see what would happen the following year.

I waited and I waited, but the flowers didn't really come. There was one tiny bloom at the top but that doesn't really count does it? I was so disappointed. Because I didn't really understand the timeframe of when things should blossom, I waited for too long to see the flower and didn't realize that damage had already been done at the root.

The damage was caused by another unassuming plant. It was planted far enough away from my hydrangea but it really grew. It thrived! In its aggressive growth it actually hindered the development of the plant I wanted to grow. I could see how at the base of my hydrangea it had become overrun by this other plant. My poor hydrangea didn't stand a chance. It didn't matter how well I watered it, or how much I fertilized it, the other plant had stopped it from producing a flower.

Because I am such a plant expert, I did the only thing I knew to do. I got rid of that flower-killing plant! Some people may call it pruning but I just up and got rid of it; the entire thing.

You know what happened the next year? The hydrangea grew, and it flowered. It may take some time for it to become a thriving hydrangea bush, and if I want the colour of the flower to change I need to pay careful attention to the soil. To grow the flower I wanted, I had to first deal with what was happening at the root.

I didn't really want to get rid of that entire unruly plant. I felt like it would be obvious I didn't really know what I was doing. The large gap where it used to be looked a bit awkward and I worried people would make fun of me. It can feel that way when we hack something right out of our lives. Especially if it's been there for a long time, or if we're known for it.

> *It can feel scary, we can feel exposed and fear what*
> *we will miss out on once that thing is gone.*

The hardest weeds to get rid of are the ones we refuse to let go of. The ones we have a "right" to, the ones we've grown up with, the ones that are uncomfortable to let go of, the ones attached to shame, pride, judgement, anger or fear. Pay attention to your feelings. Why are you angry about something? Why has this flared up? What do you need to let go of and deal with? What are you afraid to let go of?

Letting go of the things in our heart can mirror us holding on to things physically. I don't know if you've watched any shows regarding clutter or hoarding but they have become popular in the last few years. It's all fun and games and entertainment until we have to deal with something in our own house.

That Mess Tho

A few years ago I felt incredibly overrun by the clutter in our home. I was desperate to do some purging but I just didn't know how. Every time I tried, I got overwhelmed and gave up. Clutter seemed to spring up overnight and it made me feel incredibly depressed and anxious.

Miraculously, I stumbled upon a woman online who was a decluttering expert. Though I have never met this person, through her virtual encouragement and online tools I was able to look at my mess in a whole new light. She gave me the right questions to ask and as I began to purge again, I gained momentum as I was actually seeing progress. I was even able to ship the oldest kids off to their grandparents for a few nights and do an intentional deep purge from top to bottom. I could not believe how hard I worked to gut our house. I felt so much better. I was tired, but so clean and free!

Then the kids got home.

What I'd really like to understand are the physics behind how it can take you an entire day to clean the house but 20 minutes to create a disaster again! I was a little heart-broken when they returned and chaos seemed to reign once more. That night as we did a quick tidy something was different. It wasn't a bomb as I thought. Sure, they'd come in and made a mess, but all the hard work I had done actually paid off. We didn't have as much stuff kicking around so it actually didn't take much time at all to get the house put back together.

This is such a good picture of our hearts. Sometimes we can do a ton of work and feel like "Yes! I have arrived! Everything is clean and clear and I am walking freely and lightly!" Then whammo, a tornado of chaos arrives and we feel like, "Wait a minute, I just cleared that out?! Now it's a mess again!" Can I offer you a little hope here? It may feel like all is lost momentarily, but when you have partnered with Christ to remove the junk in your heart; (when you've done the "big purge") then when little things pop up they may seem heavy and tangling and hard, but they are easier to get rid of. Sure they will still take some effort on our part. There may be some confession and repentance, there may be offence you need to let go of, or you may need to ask for forgiveness. Here's the thing - you can do it! You have the tools and you are not facing the giant mess you once were.

The fact is, my house will continue to have clutter and need regular purging and maintenance because people live in it! The same is true for you and your heart. You are a living, breathing, person who is prone to wander and sin, living on a planet FULL of other broken and sinful people! It's not "if weeds get planted again" it's "when."

Just because that is the case it doesn't mean we throw in the towel and run into sin. It just means that we know what to do when we realize a weed has been planted again. Even though it is in our human nature to sin it doesn't mean we don't work to continually become more like Jesus, throwing off our sin and running our race.

> "A man reaps what he sows. Whoever sows to please their flesh, from the flesh will reap destruction; whoever sows to please the Spirit, from the Spirit will reap eternal life."
> **GALATIANS 6:7-8**

How do we unknowingly sow into our flesh? Why is it hard to plant seeds we want?

Sowing into our flesh is easy. It is comfort. It's choosing what I want to do instead of what I should do. It's holding onto that grudge because it's "Just this once." It's picking up the phone to gossip because, "I just need to vent."

This is sowing into our flesh. It is saying, "I am in pain and I need to find my own comfort," instead of running into the arms of our Comforter. It is trusting fully in ourselves instead of our Creator. Sowing into our flesh produces weeds of fear and anxiety. When we are trusting in ourselves over trusting God to come through for us, we are on the hook. We are in control. Often when I make these choices it is because I am operating out of a place of fear and lies.

> "Jesus said, "If you hold to my teaching, you are really my disciples.
> Then you will know the truth and the truth will set you free."
> **JOHN 8:31-32**

The truth will set you free and will bring you peace. Though we can't explain it, the peace that Jesus brings will displace the worry and fear in our lives. "Perfect love drives out fear." 1 John 4:18. We have Perfect Love living right inside us! But often we get in our own way. We say and do things to solve our own problems instead of allowing the One who created our souls to heal them. We may have to do heavy and hard things in the process but it is always for our good. It is always for our freedom.

> "It is for freedom that Christ has set us free. Stand firm, then, and do not let yourselves be burdened again by a yoke of slavery."
> **GALATIANS 5:1**

Just because it is hard do not give up! Do not lose heart for in due time you will reap a harvest. The enemy will use the same tactics again and again. He will use where we have failed to attach shame and make us believe we are somehow disqualified. Be aware but also remember there is grace coming directly from Jesus. When we experience salvation through a relationship with Christ, we do not instantly get a 6-pack. It takes work. Continue to invite God into your mess. Continue to invite Him into the deepest parts of your heart.

"At one time we were foolish, disobedient, deceived and enslaved by all kinds of passions and pleasures. We lived in malice and envy, being hated and hating one another. But when the kindness and love of God our Saviour appeared, he saved us, not because of righteous things we had done, but because of his mercy. He saved us through the washing of rebirth and renewal by the Holy Spirit, whom he poured out on us generously through Jesus Christ our Saviour, so that, having been justified by his grace, we might become heirs having the hope of eternal life."

TITUS 3:3-7

This is who we are!

Rebirth, in Greek, is **paliggenesia**,[34] "A radical change of mind for the better. The word often used to denote the restoration of a thing to its pristine state." And Renewal, in Greek, is **anakainōsis**,[35] "A renovation, complete change for the better."

This is us my friends. Through Jesus we are completely renovated from the inside out. And not because of anything we have done. But because of His mercy.

This is such good news. Let us not take it lightly but let it sink in deeply that everything we ever need for a full renovation is already inside us living in us through His Spirit.

"And if the Spirit of him who raised Jesus from the dead is living in you, he who raised Christ from the dead will also give life to your mortal bodies because of his Spirit who lives in you."

ROMANS 8:11

God's Spirit is alive in you! The same Spirit that raised Jesus from the dead IS IN YOU! Run with confidence my friend - you can do it! You can live this life freely and lightly. You are not alone; you have this incredible superpower of Jesus living deeply inside you.

You are now a gardener! You have the tools. This is your garden. God will do the heavy lifting; He will help identify the weeds and be the one to pull them out but you need to be intentional to maintain your garden. No one is coming along to plant and weed it for you. Protect your soil and plant well!

"I can do all things through him who strengthens me."

PHILIPPIANS 4:13 (ESV)

SONG: *"Clear the Stage"* by Jimmy Needham[36]

DISCUSSION QUESTIONS:

1) Is there a friend you hang out with that seems to bring out the worst in you? (no need to share names) Is there a way to be more intentional about conversation with them? How could you better prepare for your time together?

2) Do you fear God (afraid) or fear God (awe and wonder)? What is your view of God?

3) Is there anything you are struggling to take out of your backpack? What have you taken out of your backpack in the last few months that has helped you walk lighter?

4) What has been the most valuable tool you have learned to use when it comes to the garden of your heart?

1) Go through your Instagram, Twitter and Facebook, wherever you spend most of your time and begin to weed out people who bring out the worst in you. Are you following people you know you shouldn't? Don't allow people online to continue to influence you and plant seeds of discontentment, anger, jealousy, and self-pity. (Also - you can mute people and not completely unfollow them if you are actual friends.) Sometimes there are people who I judge when I look at their posts. I begin to think "Why did they do that or post that?" This isn't good for my heart or mind so I also choose to unfollow them. Do whatever you need to to guard your heart and mind.

2) This is your purge week! Is there anything else you are reading, watching or listening to that isn't good for your soul? I don't mean to say you only need to watch G-rated shows, but some of the things that are getting into our hearts and minds are coming through unfiltered entertainment. Trust me I know! I spent years watching scintillating garbage TV and reading books that got my heart racing. It was like eating junk food for my heart and soul. It's time to start feeding ourselves healthy things that will grow us, feed us and mature us.

3) Plant good things! We already have a praise playlist from Week 3 - now create a podcast or book list. It has been said if you want to know who you will be in five years take a look at the books you are reading now. The same can be said for podcasts and TV. So have a look at what you are reading and listening to and create something that will truly feed your soul!

4) Take an evaluation of how you're really spending your time. Are you making sure you prioritize feeding your soul? Do you have a daily and weekly time to connect with God to be still and quiet? This is the real game changer when it comes to caring for the soil of our hearts. If this is not happening regularly, figure out what you need to do to make it happen.

5) Pull out your garden picture from Lifework week 4. Place it somewhere to remind you of all that you are planting in your heart and all that you want to continue to sow.

Wholeness

I have so enjoyed being on this journey with you. Can I just say that I know at times it was hard? I know you did some big, hard and heavy things. Can I also say, I am so proud of you! This heart work is not light stuff. But you did it. Doesn't that feel good?

I wanted to share a little more here, an epilogue of sorts. You see, we have finished weeding and tending to our garden, but like any garden in life, there will always be more work to be done. There will always be more pruning and toiling. Weeds will continue to spring up, and flowers will need to be fertilized. The good news is, you now know what to do! You along with the Master Gardener are able to take care of the soil of your heart.

> "'This Temple is going to end up far better than it started out, a glorious beginning
> but an even more glorious finish: a place in which I will hand out wholeness and holiness.'
> Decree of GOD-of-the-Angel-Armies."
>
> **HAGGAI 2:9 (THE MESSAGE)**

You are God's temple (1 Corinthians 3:16) and I truly believe this for you. You will finish so much better than when you started. When you are willing to be truly honest with yourself and allow God to reveal hidden weeds, this is the point where true freedom begins. And you might find yourself still in "the process." You may be like, "Yes this was a great start but there is so much more to go." Can I say, that is okay, in fact that is more than okay, that is great! The point isn't to finish quickly, but rather to dive deep into the process and allow the Gardener to do the work.

ENDNOTES

1. Daigle, Lauren. "Rescue." *Spotify*, 7 Sept. 2018, open.spotify.com/track/7r9kOxiNDnkAg5QKqtyjVk.

2. Hanke, Zipporah. 21 Sept. 2019.

3. Holcomb, Ellie. "Wonderfully Made." *Spotify*, 27 Jan. 2017, open.spotify.com/track/5wkXQG7N7di8Vn1hTsTQLl.

4. Cultivate: Definition of Cultivate by Lexico." *Lexico Dictionaries | English*, Lexico Dictionaries, www.lexico.com/en/definition/cultivate.

5. Holcomb, Ellie. "Wonderfully Made." *Spotify*, 27 Jan. 2017, open.spotify.com/track/5wkXQG7N7di8Vn1hTsTQLl.

6. "`Aruwm." *Blue Letter Bible*, www.blueletterbible.org/lang/lexicon/lexicon.cfm?strongs=H6175

7. Lewis, C. S. *The Screwtape Letters*. Harper Collins, 2002.

8. "Kleptēs." *Blue Letter Bible*, www.blueletterbible.org/lang/lexicon/lexicon.cfm?strongs=G2812&t=kjv.

9. "Kleptō." *Blue Letter Bible*, www.blueletterbible.org/lang/lexicon/lexicon.cfm?strongs=G2813.

10. "Thyō." *Blue Letter Bible*, www.blueletterbible.org/lang/lexicon/lexicon.cfm?strongs=G2380.

11. "Apollymi." *Blue Letter Bible*, www.blueletterbible.org/lang/lexicon/lexicon.cfm?strongs=G622.

12. Hughes, John. *Home Alone*. Twentieth Century Fox, 1990.

13. Daigle, Lauren. "You Say." *Spotify*, 7 Sept. 2018, open.spotify.com/track/6Up545NUflOiXo8cEraH49.

14. Caine, Christine. "Christine Caine." *Christine Caine - I Hope Your New Year Is off to a Great...*, 2017, www.facebook.com/theChristineCaine/posts/i-hope-your-new-year-is-off-to-a-great-starti-know-the-month-is-moving-quickly-b/10158290512690089/.

15. Leaf, Caroline. "Episode #54: How to Deal with Anger and Toxic People." *Episode #54: How to Deal with Anger and Toxic People*, PodBean Development, 11 Nov. 2018, podcast.drleaf.com/e/episode-54-how-to-deal-with-anger-and-toxic-people/.

16. "Machaira." *Blue Letter Bible*, www.blueletterbible.org/lang/lexicon/lexicon.cfm?strongs=G3162.

17. Reiner, Rob, director. *The Princess Bride*. MGM Home Entertainment, 1987.

18. "Rhēma." *Blue Letter Bible*, www.blueletterbible.org/lang/lexicon/lexicon.cfm?strongs=G4487.

19. Springer, Rita. "Defender." *Spotify*, 3 Mar. 2017, open.spotify.com/track/5cPAOFa2Z1M7B6eAPWg92P.

20. "Raphah." *Blue Letter Bible*, www.blueletterbible.org/lang/lexicon/lexicon.cfm?t=kjv&strongs=h7503.

21. "Yada`." *Blue Letter Bible*, www.blueletterbible.org/lang/lexicon/lexicon.cfm?strongs=H3045.

22. Abrams, J.J. and Matt Reeves, directors. *Felicity*. WB Network, 1998.

23. for KING & COUNTRY. "Joy." *Spotify*, 5 Oct. 2018, open.spotify.com/track/0vBjd0I8iefycEZ2ex1Zpi.

24. "The Necessity of Stress." *Heads and Tales at Marin Academy*, 12 Dec. 2013, travisma.wordpress.com/2013/12/12/the-necessity-of-stress/.

25. "Dokimion." *Blue Letter Bible*, www.blueletterbible.org/lang/lexicon/lexicon.cfm?strongs=G1383.

26. "Hypomonē." *Blue Letter Bible*, www.blueletterbible.org/lang/lexicon/lexicon.cfm?strongs=G5281.

27. "How Do Palm Trees Withstand Hurricanes?" *LiveScience*, Purch, 12 Sept. 2017, www.livescience.com/60393-why-palm-trees-are-so-flexible.html.

28. "Epitimaō." *Blue Letter Bible*, www.blueletterbible.org/lang/lexicon/lexicon.cfm?strongs=G2008.

29. "New Wine." *Hillsong Worship - New Wine Official Lyrics | Lyrics*, hillsong.com/lyrics/new-wine/.

30. Torwalt, Bryan & Katie. "Praise Before My Breakthrough." *Spotify*, 16 Nov. 2018, open.spotify.com/track/48ccRS16aHgWplSvvCYQ6y

31. "Metamorphoō." *Blue Letter Bible*, www.blueletterbible.org/lang/lexicon/lexicon.cfm?strongs=G3339.

32. "Anakainōsis." *Blue Letter Bible*, www.blueletterbible.org/lang/lexicon/lexicon.cfm?strongs=G342.

33. "Ogkos." *Blue Letter Bible*, www.blueletterbible.org/lang/lexicon/lexicon.cfm?strongs=G3591.

34. "Paliggenesia." *Blue Letter Bible*, www.blueletterbible.org/lang/lexicon/lexicon.cfm?strongs=G3824.

35. "Anakainōsis." *Blue Letter Bible*, www.blueletterbible.org/lang/lexicon/lexicon.cfm?strongs=G342.

36. Needham, Jimmy. "Clear the Stage." *Spotify*, 14 May 2013, open.spotify.com/track/6GQZ5WNHhqs6b0BD0lUK96.

CPSIA information can be obtained
at www.ICGtesting.com
Printed in the USA
LVHW070110080520
655200LV00025B/115